"I have known Dr. Pitman, professionally and personally, for more than 20 years. He has strong Christian values in his personal and professional life. As a chiropractic physician, he incorporates medical science and medical intuition and responds to the patient's personal, physical, and spiritual needs. Through his care many patients have found healing, and now Dr. Pitman's insights are available to all through *The Ten Commandments of Ultimate Health*."
William A. Westendorf, DDS, MT, ND, Cincinnati, Ohio

"I had been doing my best to live a healthy lifestyle and to teach my children the same. It is difficult to maintain this in our society. After learning about the Ten Commandments of Ultimate Health program, I found it easier to continue. I had found the support that I needed and much more information to keep me moving in the right direction!"
Maria Motz, Cincinnati, Ohio

"We were desperate. We had run out of medical options. Even our doctor said she no longer knew what to do for our son's asthma. We kept adding more medications, but it didn't change the outcome. After seeing Dr. Pitman for six months, my son is much healthier, he is on fewer medications, and we are planning on eliminating more medications down the road. We are no longer desperate; now we are hopeful. Dr. Pitman has changed our life for the better, and I expect that he will impact many more lives through his book, *The Ten Commandments of Ultimate Health*."
N. Eichhold, Cincinnati, Ohio

My lifestyle has changed since I started seeing Dr. Pitman and began following what he now refers to as the Ten Commandments of Ultimate Health. I developed severe allergies in my early twenties. For the last ten to twenty years, I was using Singulair, Nasonex, and Claritan daily to cope with them. After going through NAET (Nambudripad's Allergy Elimination Technique) with Dr. Pitman, I rarely need to take any medications, and I have control of my allergies. In addition, I now avoid genetically modified foods whenever possible by going to my local and reputable farmer's market, drinking more water, exercising, and making health a priority. At the age of 43, I feel better than I ever have before.

L. Bernard, Cincinnati, Ohio

Every patient who came into my office that had been healed from health problems found relief after seeing Dr. Greg Pitman. Everyone who went to see him seemed to get well. After five years of hearing his name along with my patient's testimonials, I decided to seek him out. I was so impressed because he used twelve different methods that work extremely well together. I have found that he has the best way to identify the root causes of health problems and understands how to address the issues.

The Ten Commandments of Ultimate Health details Dr. Pitman's knowledge and spiritual insights. They will lead to a healthier life for many readers.

Dr. Robert Rothan, DDS, Cincinnati, Ohio

THE TEN COMMANDMENTS OF
ULTIMATE HEALTH

DR. GREG PITMAN, DC, DNBHE
WITH LYNN THESING

Carpenter's Son Publishing

TABLE OF CONTENTS

PART THREE

REFERENCES

ACKNOWLEDGMENTS

I want to thank God for all he has done in my life and for the patients he has entrusted to my hands. I am blessed and honored to serve God's people. I have great appreciation for the courageous testimonies of my patients and their sharing of their respective journeys of healing.

Most of all, I thank my wonderful wife, Donna, and my children, Gregory, Mikayla, and Grant. Donna is a blessing to me from God and is the love of my life. She has been a great gift to me and has taught me sacrificial love that I would have never known without her. We have made many sacrifices together to raise our family and work on this book. My children have taught me many things in the journey of raising them. I thank God for them.

I am very thankful to Lynn Thesing for her writing and the support she has given to me. Without her spiritual gift of writing and her insights, this book would not have been possible. I thank God for Lynn; as a team, we have chance to help many hurting people in this world. This is a book to help those who desire to achieve ultimate healing in their lives.

— *Dr. Greg Pitman, DC, DNBHE*

Thanks to God, my supportive and loving husband, Jim, my children, parents, and sisters, and to Dr. Pitman, for giving my family our lives back and allowing me to spread the word to others.

— *Lynn Thesing*

TESTIMONIAL BY FORD TAYLOR

I was born and raised in Texas. My first business ventures were to buy broken companies and turn them around. This process took place through the 80's and 90's and led to a group that grew a company to an approximately $300 million publicly traded apparel business. I found myself in the position of CEO.

Through a series of events, I moved to Cincinnati to work with a new business acquisition. I commuted from Texas to Cincinnati for just under two years. During this time, I fell into a life of adultery, a lifestyle counter to everything I knew and believed in.

My family life looked perfect, but my sinful lifestyle and frequent travel schedule was taking a toll on both my marriage and my health. What the outside world didn't see was a severely depressed man, one who had everything the world had to offer, yet a man on the verge of a total mental breakdown—and suicide. I had lost my way in every area, including my faith in God.

Around this same time, I volunteered to coach my child's soccer team with another parent, Dan. During a practice, I dove for a ball and hurt my ribs. Over the next few weeks, I used a heating pad, and Dan used every chance he had to encourage me to see Dr. Pitman.

I had no inclination to see him. The more Dan talked about Dr. Pitman and the various "treatments" he offered, the more resolved I was to never step foot in his practice. I wrote off Dr. Pitman as "crazy" and went about my heating pad therapy.

I had been to another doctor about my ailing ribs. I was told that an X-ray was unwarranted because it would not change the treatment plan. If they were broken, they would heal in three weeks, he said. If they were bruised, it would be six weeks.

When I was still in pain three months later, Dan booked an

appointment for me at Dr. Pitman's office. After meeting Dr. Pitman at a dinner party, I decided it probably couldn't hurt to appease Dan, and I went to the appointment.

I had a complete initial exam with X-rays. I was sitting on the chiropractic table, and Dr. Pitman came in and sat down next to me. "I want you to put your arm around me," Dr. Pitman said. "Look, buddy, we just met," I joked. "No, I want you to put your arm around me," he said. So I put my arm around him, and Dr. Pitman reached over and put his arm all the way around my back, placing his hands near my rib cage. Then Dr. Pitman said, "Now, I want you to lean over on my hand, and I want you to take a deep breath. Then when I tell you to, I want you throw yourself on me and blow out." I thought, That's crazy. But I did it anyway.

I reluctantly did this three times. Then Dr. Pitman said, "Now stand up and take a breath." I stood and took a small breath, as I had done for the last three months. Dr. Pitman encouraged me to take a full breath. And when I did, there was no pain.

"What did you do?!" I asked. Dr. Pitman explained that my ribs were not broken or bruised. They were dislocated.

I started regular visits with Dr. Pitman. During one of these visits, Dr. Pitman sensed that my liver was distressed. He asked how long I had been fighting depression. I asked, "How do you know I have depression?" His reply: "I can feel it in your liver." "What do you mean you can you feel it in my liver?" I asked. Dr. Pitman said, "I can just feel it."

A little while later, he asked, "So what kind of antidepressants are you taking?" "How do you know I am taking antidepressants?" I asked. "I can feel them in your system," he said. Man you are crazy! I thought.

Dr. Pitman asked, "Would you let me treat your liver?" I said, "Do I have to believe it will work for it to work?" He told me that I did not. So I said, "Than you can do anything you want." Dr. Pitman looked at me and said, "Ford, did you know that when your body, mind, and spirit are aligned, you can hear God in ways you never thought possible?" I left there thinking Dr. Pitman was the craziest person I had ever known.

In high school, I was so in touch with Jesus and fired up for God. I knew I was meant for God's kingdom, yet I walked away from the calling that I knew was on my life. I continued on into my current adulterous lifestyle while looking to the outside world as if I had the "God thing" going on. But, in truth, I didn't. And I didn't think I could get it back.

Now, suddenly, there was this most unconventional — if not crazy — doctor who was telling me that if I got my body, spirit, and mind in alignment, I would be able to hear from God in ways I never imagined. What a strange thing for a doctor to say to a guy, I thought.

I continued along my protocol of supplements and chiropractic visits, and within a short amount of time, my depression was gone. I was now visiting Dr. Pitman's office three times a week. At the beginning of my treatment, I was taking medicine for reflux, spastic colon, antidepressants, and anxiety; I was regularly taking three rosacea medicines and allergy medicines.

On my own, I stopped taking my antidepressants, not knowing that stopping them suddenly wasn't a good thing to do. One day Dr. Pitman said, "Oh, your depression's gone." I replied that I was aware of this. I explained that I had stopped taking the medicine. Dr. Pitman was very concerned that I had stopped the medications suddenly, and he explained that these medicines had to be slowly taken out of the body.

I agreed to go to my psychiatrist and tell her what I had done. When the appointment time came, I walked into her office and she said, "What happened to you?" I shared that I had been healed of the depression. The psychiatrist said, "That's not possible," because of my family history of depression. She told me that when the antidepressants ran through my system, I would be back for more medicine. I told her that I had been off the pills for three months, so they had already run through my system. It has been almost ten years, and I have never been back on meds for depression again.

I continued my aggressive schedule of three visits per week with Dr. Pitman. I was treated with NAET (Nambudripad's Allergy Elimination Technique) for my allergies (you'll read much more about NAET treatments — which start with autonomic reflex testing to determine whether certain allergens are in the body — throughout this book). I had nutrition appointments, using biofeedback, and took all the supplements Dr. Pitman prescribed. During this time, I went to see my mother in Texas. She noticed I was not using my standard "box of Kleenex" like I typically did. My allergies were going away. To prove my point, I picked up a family cat, placed it on my face, and inhaled. After that display, my mother traveled north to Cincinnati to find her own healing with Dr. Pitman.

Little by little, I was able to reduce and eventually eliminate all the medicines I was taking. As my physical healing was progressing, God started working on my spiritual healing as well.

I was at a meeting with two other Christian leaders, Dale and Anita Thorne. Anita caught me off guard, asking, "Ford, if you knew you were doing what God called you to do, what would you do?"

I was able to share with them that I had received a calling from God back in high school, but I could not interpret what the call meant. God had called me again years later, but corporate opportunities lured me from the calling once again. But there in that room, I knew I had to share what I felt God had been calling me to do for decades.

"I guess if I was doing what God called me to do, I would stop hiding behind words like integrity and morality and I'd probably talk about Jesus more," I answered. Then I sarcastically added, "Who knows? Maybe I'd even go to seminary. Maybe I'd even preach some." Dale answered: "Why don't you do that?" And I felt ashamed and replied: "Because God doesn't talk to me anymore. There's a reason he doesn't talk to me anymore."

Anita asked, "Can we pray?" When she started praying, the power of the Holy Spirit filled the room. As she prayed, I sensed the same words, in my mind, that she spoke moments before she spoke them.

God was calling me one last time to do his work. This time God made the calling on my life public and surrounded me with Dale and Anita to help me walk out his calling.

Dale quipped, "So, God doesn't speak to you anymore?" I replied, "Well, I guess I just don't listen. But there is a reason." I walked out of that meeting a changed man. I broke off my adulterous lifestyle and really started seeking and asking God what he wanted me to do.

I began to understand that God wanted me to utilize my leadership skills to change communities. I cofounded Transformation Cincinnati & Northern Kentucky, a nonprofit group with the mission to facilitate the uniting of God's people in businesses, churches, families, government, communities, ministries, and schools locally and beyond.

I think I got such quick results with Dr. Pitman because he helped me to heal physically as well as mentally, emotionally, and spiritually. I believe I was able to hear and act on God's call because my mind, body, soul, and spirit were aligned.

> Until we change the way we think, we are not going to change the way we feel. If we keep thinking the way we have always thought, then we are going to keep feeling the way we have always felt.

I have sent many people to Dr. Pitman. I tell them that, "it is weird, but it is time for a change." Until we change the way we think, we are not going to change the way we feel. If we keep thinking the way we have always thought, then we are going to keep feeling the way we have always felt. If we keep feeling the way we have always felt, we will keep acting the way we have always acted.

I believe my physical healing has created a domino effect. Through my healing, God used Dr. Pitman to turn me back to Christ, and I have been able to help others find their way back to Jesus through my failures and healing. Jesus tells us that the most important thing that we can do is to love God with all our heart, mind, soul, and flesh (spiritually, mentally, emotionally, and physically), and that the Second Commandment is like the first: to love others as we love ourselves.

God used Dr. Pitman to change my life. Now it is your turn. Be courageous enough to take a chance on thinking differently.

— *Ford Taylor*

Ford Taylor owns FSH Consulting Group, which is led by a team that provides leadership training, strategic consulting, and executive coaching. His desire is to see individuals and teams achieve transformation by addressing and removing personal and professional constraints. He resides with his wife, Sandra, and one daughter in Cincinnati, and has two other daughters in college.

PART ONE

MY STORY: SEARCHING FOR HEALING

Everyone has a number of defining moments in his or her life. One of mine came at the age of 13. My body was going through enough changes, but now my heart was shattered by the death of my grandfather.

Without my grandfather, I felt alone and angry. My grandfather was everything to me. He invested time, energy, and part of himself in me. We went on hunting and fishing trips where he would listen, give advice, and share his wisdom with me. Now, he was gone. A heavy depression was setting in.

Four months prior, we were on a trip together, getting ready for a day of fishing. As we were loading the boat into the water, my grandfather slipped and broke a rib. He was taken to the hospital, where doctors discovered that he not only had a broken rib, he also had leukemia. Since blood transfusions were the only remedy for leukemia in the 1970s, my grandfather received one. He mentioned that his arm felt like it was burning as the blood went in. Later in my training, I would learn that he had reacted to something during that procedure. He died the next day. He was only 59 years old.

The week before his death, I was a boy who dreamed of being an architect, but the day he died, everything changed. I remember lying on the bathroom floor, weak from grief and days of crying, asking: *How can this happen? He was healthy. How can he be gone? What about me? How will I make it without him?* Then I asked even tougher questions, ones that would change my life forever: *Why did he pass away? . . . He was still fairly young. Could his death have been prevented?*

I didn't know God at the time, but he had set the stage for the journey into my own healing, ultimately to be used to heal others.

Before that could happen, I experienced more sickness: German measles, allergies, asthma, inflammation, and obesity. I couldn't breathe when I went outside due to the asthma, and this impacted my social life, isolating me from others. I was miserable. I was taking a multitude of drugs, antibiotics, and shots. At the age of 13, my body was overwhelmed by allergens, and I broke out with a staph infection. I had boils on every part of my body. To "cure" the boils, my doctor had to drain them. I remember lying on the doctor's table, covered in boils, as the doctor drained them with his bare hands. The intensity of the pain was so sharp and nauseating that I eventually passed out. When I woke up, and later as I learned more, I realized that this procedure was not just torturous, it was an archaic and medieval form of medicine. There had to be a better way.

I was angry that I had to be exposed to such painful procedures. I was angry that nothing was working. I was mad at doctors and their lack of ability to help me, and I was really angry that my grandfather had been taken away. I was angry that my body was sick and that I had to live with physical pain. I was angry!

These deep emotions propelled my journey to find answers and

> The week before his death I was a boy who dreamed of being an architect, but the day he died, everything changed.

healing. I completed eight years of schooling — my undergraduate work at Bluffton University and my chiropractic program at Palmer College — in just six years. I took classes every summer, worked extremely hard, and fatigued myself searching for answers. I had a passion to understand the body . . . the physiology, biology, mechanics, and the physics (energy) involved with it.

After graduating from chiropractic college, I was still sick. I knew chiropractic care was going to be a part of my healing, but I also knew that there was more. I began to travel throughout Europe and other parts of the world, searching for more ways to help my body be free of allergies and illness.

In the United States, we don't usually understand the natural medicine techniques that are being used to achieve healing in other countries. But I had an opportunity to learn many different protocols, ones rarely utilized in the States. Everything I learned worked as a complement to chiropractic care. I worked diligently for the first three weeks of every month so I could afford to travel to more training at the end of the month. During all this searching and learning I stumbled upon NAET (Nambudripad's Allergy Elimination Technique), and I will expand on it throughout the book. It utilizes acupressure, a noninvasive form of acupuncture, to eliminate any type of sensitivity or allergy.[1] I have had tremendous success with it both personally and professionally. It was critical in my healing process, and I have treated many others using this technique. I consider it one of the key components to healing.

During this time, I also discovered Electro Dermal Screening (EDS). EDS utilizes a probe on an acupuncture meridian to measure the galvanic current. I test the meridians on a patient's joints, hands, and feet to assess changes in the current that can indicate illness. This offers a tool to address the root cause of a patient's symptoms.

In addition, I spent hundreds of hours studying homeopathy, broadening my understanding of how the natural substances, given to us by God, can provide remedies for the body. I have found homeopathy to be more effective than most modern pharmaceuticals.

After all of my travels, I had a huge understanding of how the body works. I now understood how I needed to change my life in order to achieve ultimate health, and I began to incorporate these changes into daily living habits. All of these experiences gave me the intellectual foundation of my practice. This way of life has become what I call the Ten Commandments of Ultimate Health.

WALK TO EMMAUS

The human body is comprised of physical, mental, and emotional systems that work together. You are only as healthy or strong as your weakest body system. While my body was being healed, my knowledge of the physical, emotional, and mental systems was being transformed. I continued to heal myself throughout my mid-20s.

At 27, I accepted Christ in my life. You may have heard the stories of people giving their lives to Christ or "becoming saved" — and everything comes together for them. For many, this spiritual time also becomes a time of challenge, filled with events that test the new relationship with Christ. During this time I was challenged — and failed by giving into many temptations. This time of challenge helped me understand that the support of other Christians is vital to leading a life that is pleasing to God. I met my wife Donna two years later. Very soon after meeting her, I knew she was the one who God intended for me.

When we first met, Donna was having significant hair loss. She had been to numerous doctors and was using cortisone on her scalp to try to alleviate the problem, but it was not improving. After learning that she was still grieving from the death of her grandmother, I suggested that her thyroid gland was probably not functioning properly due to the grief, and that this could be causing the hair loss. I recommended supplementation, and Donna's hair stopped falling out. This experience, combined with her very holistic upbringing on a farm, helped prepare her for the unusual but effective practices I used every day. With her support, I continued to study and build a successful practice.

Around the age of 37, I had the opportunity to go on a spiritual retreat called the Walk to Emmaus. I believe God has always been with me, even as a little child, guiding my steps. But just as I had to travel to other countries to gain further medical knowledge, my Walk to Emmaus deepened my understanding and relationship with Christ.

> Up until this retreat, I had been running at full speed chasing after knowledge about the human body and healing process. At Emmaus, I slowed down just long enough to hear God.

Up until this retreat, I had been running at full speed chasing after knowledge about the human body and healing process. At Emmaus, I slowed down just long enough to hear God. In the years since my grandfather's death, anger fueled my insatiable drive for intellectual knowledge. At Emmaus, I began to understand how deeply God desired healing. Not only the healing of people's physical bodies, but of their emotional scars, sinful natures, and past wounds.

One night at the Walk to Emmaus, God spoke to me throughout the night: "You know that anger has been used to help you. Anger propelled you to grow and motivated you to keep going. It was used to push you. I gave you this anger. It was good at the time. It motivated you to go beyond your own dreams, beyond where most people normally go. I put this passion in your heart. The anger in your life caused you to seek out knowledge. It has allowed you to go out into the future. It motivated you to keep going and push you to where you are today. I planted the desire in your heart to help and heal people. But this anger is no longer good. You've used this anger, and now you're done with it. You need to stop the anger inside you and be peaceful."

God speaks to people in so many different ways. We are each unique, and we receive God's individual message for us in varying ways. For me, I knew it was time to leave my anger behind and put my knowledge and training into action. Making the connection between the way I was living and the anger was significant. I hadn't realized that I was still carrying this anger around. Now that I did, I was able to give it to God, realizing that my grandfather was in a better place and that there really is a plan. Relying on scripture as a reminder of God's plan and promises was also helpful during this time.

Just as I was challenged when I first accepted Christ, I was also challenged after the Walk to Emmaus. The next few years proved to be rocky, but the difficulties caused me to get to know the Lord at a deeper level. God provided experiences in my life that caused me to grow, learn, and lean on him.

Finding God's Plan for Healing

I have found that as people achieve physical healing, they grow closer to God. It is through their healing that they are made more fully available to be used by God for his purposes.

In my reading, I looked in the Bible and found many references on how to live a healthy life; these principles became the foundation for this book. What I began to call the Ten Commandments of Ultimate Health helped to bring my body into balance and allowed me to achieve the life I wanted. In my practice, I see many people who have horrible health issues, and many of these issues could be avoided by incorporating healthy, daily living habits into their lives.

When we are feeling our best, then we are able to do the work of the Lord at a deeper level. If you feel bad much of the time, you are not going to go grow with Christ as you should. You may not have the strength, energy, or ability to fulfill the purposes that God has created for you.

If everyone followed these principles — the Ten Commandments of Ultimate Health — we would be a healthier nation. Instead, we are a sick nation, one in which our children are challenged by epidemics of diabetes, cancer, obesity, autism, asthma, allergies, and ADHD. In my practice, I am seeing an alarming and unprecedented number of children with these conditions. Adults are also plagued with an alarming rate of countless other diseases, including IBS (Irritable Bowel Syndrome), Crohn's disease, multiple sclerosis, and many types of cancer.

> **In our physical suffering we learn a lot about God and a lot about ourselves.**

We are beaten down by all the sickness, disease, and illness in the world. In order to combat the many things that cause us to be sick in the world and to begin to heal, we have to begin to think differently from the thought patterns of the world. I have adopted this passage, in Romans 12:2, as the foundation of my life:

> *Do not conform any longer to the pattern of this world, but be transformed by the renewing of your mind. Then you will be able to test and approve what God's will is — his good, pleasing and perfect will.*

This verse continues to speak to me on a daily basis. We are all called to be living sacrifices for God. We need to be equipped for God to be able to use us. This book is a guide for you to prepare your body at a deeper level so that you may be used by God to reach out to others. We are called not to conform to this world of illness but to be transformed *by the renewing of our minds.*

In our physical suffering we learn a lot about God and a lot about ourselves. I feel I suffered so much as a child to learn these truths and to share them with others. Perhaps your suffering is not just for yourself but also for you to learn from and share with others.

This book will give you new information. Some of it may be challenging for you to accept, but in order to achieve true wellness and healing, you may need to make some foundational shifts in the way you think.

TRADITIONAL MEDICINE

Patients often call my treatments alternative medicine, but I prefer the term "traditional medicine," since many of these practices date back to biblical times.

The World Health Organization (WHO), in an online report titled "Traditional Medicine," wrote: "Traditional medicine has been used for thousands of years with great contributions made by practitioners to human health . . . " Traditional medicine includes herbal medicine, acupuncture/acupressure, manipulation, and massage.

Traditional medicine has not stood still over the last thousand years. It has progressed, using centuries of knowledge combined with state-of-the-art technology to provide more effective healing treatments than ever before. Today's homeopath can provide supplements that protect against one's genetic taints after having DNA analyzed through saliva. Today's traditional practitioners use highly advanced tools, like thermography, which measures heat patterns and can detect an abnormality or change in the body. *Modern medicine* is another term often used to describe today's conventional medicine, but the traditional medicine that I practice is not ancient medicine only. While it has its roots in the practices of the ancients, it is also technologically advanced.

Conventional medicine treats symptoms. By covering the symptoms, the patient receives immediate results and often feels better for a period of time. But it is often a temporary fix, treating the symptoms but not addressing the underlying problems. The symptoms are resolved in a day or week, but the illness is still present and is likely to cause worse issues down the road. Traditional medicine treats the underlying problem, but the symptoms are not eliminated as quickly. True physical healing takes time, but the perseverance needed is worth it because it resolves *the cause* of the illness, not just *the symptoms.*

> Traditional medicine has not stood still over the last thousand years. It has progressed, using centuries of knowledge combined with state-of-the-art technology to provide more effective healing treatments than ever before.

Many people either do not believe in or do not take advantage of traditional medicine until they are "broken." I believe that societal resistance to traditional medicine stems from looking for the quick fix instead of taking the proper time needed to actually heal. Often, before someone steps foot in my office, they have already tried conventional medicine consisting of potentially damaging pharmaceuticals, unnecessary surgeries, and dashed hopes. They have nowhere else to turn. They are broken. If individuals would open themselves to traditional medicine before being "broken," they could be saved from unnecessary heartache and expense.

WHY ARE WE SICK?

Why are we sick? It's not bad genes. It's not bad luck. It's bad living habits! Genetics is what we're born with. And to some extent, our genetics predispose us to be more susceptible to certain diseases. However, *what cannot be changed can often be controlled.*

Epigenetics is the study of how genes express themselves. Studies are showing that genes can be changed through lifestyle choices. Good diet and supplementation can actually change your genes for the better. Poor diet and lack of supplementation have the ability to make your predisposition to certain diseases worse.[2]

Epigenetic scientists have proven that extreme environmental conditions and stressors can cause a "mark" that sits on top of the genome, your full set of chromosomes that contains all traits you have inherited. This mark tells your gene to be dominant or recessive. It essentially turns the gene on or off for one or more generations. It has already been shown that extreme starvation followed by overabundance of food will cause an epigenetic mark that shortens the offspring's life by up to 32 years![3]

This "gene marking" does not change your DNA. It does, however, change how your body and the bodies of your offspring process life as it happens. Epigenetics also lends itself to supplementation. Deficiencies may trigger a genetic marker.[4] There are deficiencies in regard to the nutrition we take into our bodies, and in enzymes, and these depletions cause disease. Each body's genetic weaknesses are revealed when exposed to an illness. Within our genetic code, there are markers that indicate how disease will manifest itself.

This explains why one person exposed to an allergen gets a rash while another has an asthma attack. Understanding your genetic disposition will help you decipher how your body responds to disease and how to achieve healing more quickly. However, we can control our genetic predisposition by engaging in healthy living habits on a daily basis.

> Understanding your genetic disposition will help you decipher how your body responds to disease and how to achieve healing more quickly.

For the most part, we can control the genetics we are born with by following these Ten Commandments of Ultimate Health and by avoiding morbific stimuli. Morbific stimuli are those things most dangerous to your health and that should be avoided. This book is divided into two main parts following this opening section. First, I'm going to explain the Ten Commandments of Ultimate Health, the practices we must engage in to be healthy. But the final part of this book is just as important; it explains and details morbific stimuli. It provides suggestions on how to avoid the many harmful things and how to rise above the patterns of the world.

GETTING STARTED: NOTES FROM A GHOSTWRITER

Dear Reader,

It was only three years ago that I was in deep despair. My 18-month-old son, Nathan, seemed to be allergic to everything he touched. I was lost in the world of conventional medicine, spending thousands of dollars, with no results. I could see what these allergic reactions were doing to him on the outside, from gasping for air, to eczema, to horrendous gut pain. I could only imagine what they were doing to his physiological systems inside. Night after night, I watched him suffer with no relief. After receiving Dr. Pitman's name, I decided to try his traditional medicinal techniques. Within weeks, Nathan was doing better and on his way to total healing.

Not only was my youngest son sick, but my three-year-old son, Noah, also had numerous problems, including sensory integration issues, auditory processing and speech delays, and visual processing issues. I was sick as well. I was on conventional medicine for ADHD, constantly sick with a cold, and headed into depression. My entire family needed help. After being treated by Dr. Pitman, I began to question my daily living habits and started to write about our journey toward healing.

When Dr. Pitman asked me to help him write this book, I never imagined speaking in my own voice as well. However, throughout the writing process it became clear that there were going to be many readers like I had been — those people starting from scratch. You will be reading the wisdom provided by Dr. Pitman throughout the chapters of the book and will hear my voice in the Getting Started sections at the end of each chapter. These sections are designed to provide you with the perspective of one sick family making efforts toward a healthy future.

Today, three years later, we are much healthier. Nathan, now five, is allergy free. Noah, now seven, is healthy and thriving without the speech, auditory processing, or visual issues that he struggled with at such an early age. In fact, he is performing ahead of where he needs to be. I have lost 40 pounds, am no longer taking any conventional medications, and have no other health complaints. I am so happy and grateful for this amazing healing, and I rejoice every day.

Even after experiencing this astonishing healing journey, I am far from perfect. The ways of the world around me often seep into my life and move me off my healing track. My children are becoming more and more susceptible to the marketing messages that promote unhealthy lifestyles, and they want to purchase foods that their friends eat. I am constantly trying to choose my battles with regard to food.

I know that this book has become a resource for me. Reading just a few pages can set me back on track, encouraging me to tweak something in my family's lifestyle that can lead to a healthier, happier life. I hope this book can provide the same guidance to you.

Many Blessings,

Lynn Thesing
Cincinnati, Ohio

PART TWO

FIRST COMMANDMENT:
PRAY

"Do not be anxious about anything, but in every situation, by prayer and petition, with thanksgiving, present your requests to God." (Philippians 4:6)

"Listen to me and I will explain to you." (Job 15:17)

"But God has surely listened and has heard my prayer." (Psalm 66:19)

Why do we pray? We pray to be at one with our Creator, and we humble ourselves to his majesty.

Praying together can be even more powerful than by oneself. "Wherever two or more of you are gathered in my name, I am in the midst of them" (Matthew 18:20). Prayer can bring in miracles that we can see and experience. We may pray for something and expect an immediate response, but God will answer in a way that is totally in his grace. God calls us to pray each and every day, and prayer can make our world a better place.

I can remember the day I had to make a decision to move my office. I had been contemplating this for a year or more, and I was still not at peace with a decision. One early morning, I prayed to God, "Please close the doors that need to be closed and open the doors that need to be opened in order to help me find the right location for my office."

I was working with a prominent builder in the area who had a reputation for being a fiercely competitive, relentless, "get-the-deal-done" businessman. After asking God to guide me, I received a phone call from the builder. "Greg," he said, "I really think the office park on Cornell is the best place for you." It was an office park owned by his competition. In one phone call, after more than a year of working with me, this business-savvy, money-motivated builder gave up a million-dollar sale and instead pointed me to his chief competitor. I believe that God spoke through the heart of this builder, inspiring him to turn down the deal with me in order to help my business prosper. Miracles, through prayer, truly do happen every day.

I pray for healing, for myself, my family, and for my patients. In 2004, William Cromie at the Harvard University Gazette posted an article, "One-Third of Americans Pray for their Health"; the piece had the following statistics[5]:

- 35 percent of people in the United States ask a higher power to help with their health
- 75 percent of these people pray to stay healthy
- 22 percent pray for relief of just about everything (from back pain to cancer to headaches to heart problems)
- 69 percent found that praying was helpful
- Many gave higher ratings to their prayers than to their doctors

> I sometimes think that we just don't think to pray for our health until we are ill. I've been guilty of this.

I sometimes think that we just don't think to pray for our health until we are ill. I've been guilty of this. When my son Grant was born, it was an extremely difficult birth; he swallowed meconium-stained amniotic fluid. For three days, we kept vigil by him in intensive care. My wife nursed him every hour or two; neither of us slept. I was so frustrated. With my training and education, I usually knew what to do to help those who are sick, but I was completely helpless with my own son. I was sleep-deprived and completely broken when I finally had the idea to . . . pray. It was 2:30 in the morning and I prayed with my wife; we asked God to heal my son. During the prayer, I felt as if a light had come into the room. I could feel God's healing power through my entire body. In that same moment I saw my son, for the first time, take a breath without a struggle. Grant was instantly healed, right there in my wife's arms.

I am a man of faith. So why did I have to be completely broken to say a prayer? It may be that I had to give up control and let go of my own will. We sometimes have to experience this brokenness before we truly surrender to him. I believe God blessed me with this experience so that I can continue to feel his unending love and to allow me to witness his miraculous ability to heal. I can now provide testimony to my patients struggling with their own health issues, and I often pray with them.

I have incorporated prayer into my daily life and my practice. I have a prayer request box in my waiting room, and my staff and I pray for the needs of my patients. I begin everyday with the prayer of Jabez.

> *Jabez cried out to the God of Israel, "Oh, that you would bless me and enlarge my territory! Let your hand be with me, and keep me from harm so that I will be free from pain." And God granted his request. (1 Chronicles 4:10)*

Enlarging your territory may mean a less stressful job, stronger relationships, or better health. Whatever it is, we need to ask for God's guidance. Sometimes we are so stuck in the muck that we actually forget to ask God for what we need. We need to remember: "Ask and it will be given to you, seek and you will find, knock and the door will be opened to you" (Luke 11:9, 10).

There is a reason why prayer is the first commandment of ultimate health. Prayer is as vital to a healthy life as food and water, and this act of connection with God is extremely important when trying to incorporate the other nine ultimate health commandments into your life. Becoming healthy in an unhealthy world is a challenge, but "we can do all things through Christ who strengthens us" (Philippians 4:13). Taking time to pray and read the Bible should become a habit. It is the foundation needed to achieve all of the commandments of ultimate health, and it can lead to a healthier, happier life.

Getting Started

When my 18-month-old son was very sick, I was in such deep despair that I could hardly pray. I always understood that prayer plus faith could be a powerful combination. However, during this difficult time, I could hardly muster the energy to pray and had little faith that a miracle would happen to me.

I was reminded of the biblical story of the paralytic.

The paralytic had four faithful friends who carried him to Jesus, going to great lengths to see him touch their friend (Mark 2:1-12).

The fact that the paralytic was carried by more than one individual became significant to me. I called my mother and my two sisters and said, "There are four of us. I need you to carry my son to Jesus to be healed, in the same way that the four friends carried the paralytic in the Bible story." I explained that I, alone, did not have the faith. I asked them to have the faith for me, believing that my child would be healed.

Talk about pressure . . . but they agreed and prayed daily, on the phone and individually. I then called or emailed just about every person of faith that I knew, even television evangelists, churches, and cloistered convents. Knowing that all of these people were praying helped to restore my faith. Within one week, Dr. Pitman's name was given to me from two different sources, and my son began his path to healing.

If you are having a hard time getting started in your prayer life, reach out to someone who can carry you in faith. Here are the two practicals I want to give:

• Contact a volunteer working for a church, if you haven't attended for a while, or a faith-based social service agency, or even a TV or

radio ministry. Ask them to add your need to their prayer list.
- *Having prayer partners can ignite or reignite your faith. Set up a prayer partner relationship. Due to logistics, I often pray with my prayer partners over the phone. These relationships will strengthen your faith in remarkable ways.*

SECOND COMMANDMENT:
DRINK WATER

"Draw water for the siege, strengthen your defenses!"
(Nahum 3:14)

"Come, all who are thirsty, come to the waters." (Isaiah 55:1)

"From there they continued on to Beer, the well where the Lord said to Moses, 'Gather the people together and I will give them water.'" (Numbers 21:16)

In Kenya, women walk more than five hours a day to get clean drinking water for their families. The walk takes up most of their day. Young girls often drop out of school, significantly shortening their education, to help their mothers on the difficult daily journey for water. The quest for water dominates daily life.

In the United States, we have many options to obtain clean drinking water, yet many people are still thirsting and don't even realize it. Our bodies are thirsty for more water and without it we cannot detoxify, heal, or function as we should. The average human cannot be without water for more than five days before serious health issues develop, but can live five to seven weeks without food.

Water is essential for life. Your muscles are 70 percent water. Lack of water can be responsible for arthritis, back pain, skin issues, sleep, and digestive issues. You must consider your weight to truly quench your body with water. You should drink half your body weight in ounces of water each day. The average American man weighs 191 pounds and should be drinking 95.5 ounces of water daily—or one and a half gallons—and the average women weighs 164 pounds and should be drinking 82 ounces of water.

I also instruct my patients that they need to add in even more water if they are drinking coffee or other caffeinated substances as these drinks dehydrate the body. For every eight ounces of caffeine they drink, they should add an additional eight ounces of water above and beyond their standard daily amount. Coffee actually pulls water from your tissues. When combined with cream and sugar, it dehydrates our tissues even more. I recommend that my patients drink one cup of water for every cup of coffee they drink, two cups if they add sugar to the coffee, and three cups if they add creamer. There is no replacement for water. Drinking pop, tea, juice, or milk does not count toward the amount of water you require daily.

At the beginning, drinking all of this water feels like work, and it is. However, the benefits to the body are tremendous. Water distributes nutrients and vitamins throughout our systems and allows us to dump toxins. Patients report feeling energized, clearheaded, and having experienced less aches and pains as their bodies begins to rehydrate.

Clean Water

Although we don't have to walk hours to obtain clean water, we do have to do more than simply turn on the faucet. I advise my patients to get a reverse osmosis water filtration system. I have installed one at my home and at my office. Reverse osmosis was originally designed to eliminate salt from water and is the best way to bring water to its natural, colorless, odorless, and tasteless state.

According to Duke University, citing a Ralph Nader-sponsored report, our water has more than 2,110 components in it, contaminants like lead, asbestos, chlorine, and trihalomethanes.[6] It also contains hormones, medications, and other toxins.[7] I find it fascinating that every pet store employee across America knows that goldfish can't be placed in tap water because they will die, but we don't question putting it into to our own bodies.

The Kaiser Foundation reports that from 1994 to 2005 the number of prescriptions purchased in America increased 71 percent (from 2.1 billion to 3.6 billion). Where are all of these medications going? They don't simply stay in the body of the person that took them. They come out through urine and fecal matter and eventually find their way into our water.[8] According to *Medical News Today* (2008), "Officials in Philadelphia said in testing [that] they discovered 56 pharmaceuticals and by-products in treated drinking water including medicines for pain, infection, high cholesterol, asthma, epilepsy, mental illness, and heart problems."[9]

Environmental pollution also threatens the safety of our drinking water. A 2009 National Geographic investigation found not only hormones and drugs in U.S. drinking water, but also discovered rocket fuel in four percent of the water.[10]

You can access information about the safety of the water in your area at http://water.epa.gov. Do not be surprised if you find viruses and bacteria that come from human and animal fecal waste floating around in tap water. In the Ohio area, where my practice is, the EPA report findings of antimony, arsenic, asbestos, cyanide, mercury, and nitrates from fertilizer runoff.

Even the additives purposely placed into water can be toxic. A 2010 PR Newswire report said that a study in two Chinese villages demonstrated that 28 percent of children in low-fluoride areas were found to be "bright and of normal or higher" intelligence as compared with just eight percent in higher fluoride areas. In the high-fluoride area, 15 percent had scores indicating mental retardation compared with only six percent in the low fluoride area. This study controlled for other factors like lead, iodine, and other brain-damaging toxins and diseases.[11]

The EPA (http://water.epa.gov/drink/local/) warns that fluoride can cause bone disease and mottled teeth in children.[12] Hmmm . . .

isn't fluoride supposed to be helping our teeth?

My biological dentist recommends using nonfluoridated toothpaste like Spry or Thom's of Maine with xylitol, and I have found it to be a good way to prevent tooth decay. Consistently, research supports the use of xylitol for the prevention of tooth decay, but the use of fluoride has recently been in question. A 2010 *Science Daily* report actually found that the protective shield of fluoride is 100 times thinner than previously believed and raises the question of whether it can prevent cavities.[13]

The reverse osmosis filtration system will remove fluoride and other such toxins from the water and is a relatively inexpensive option for most patients.

Bottled Water and Storage Issues

If you are going to purchase bottled water, be careful that you are actually paying for water that has been purified by a reverse osmosis system. Many times individuals pay for water that comes from a spring that is not regulated or from another municipality source (tap water).

How your water is stored can also make a huge difference in its impact on your health. Avoid plastic containers as they are high in benzene, halogen, and bromine. These compounds block the endocrine system and cause neurological damage.

The National Toxicology Program (NTP) committee agreed that bisphenol A (BPA), a chemical found in polycarbonate (used to make water cooler jugs, sport-water bottles, and other hard plastics) causes neurological and behavioral problems in fetuses, babies, and children.

In addition, adult exposure to BPA likely affects the brain and the female reproductive system.[14] BPA is still found today in plastics with the recycled number seven.

When using reverse osmosis bottled water, you need to be aware of where you store it. Storing bottled water in your garage, car, or other storage place that is not temperature-regulated can cause the chemicals in the plastics to leak into your drinking water.

When a patient is having a hard time drinking the amount of water they need (remember: half your body weight in ounces), I usually suspect that they're drinking tap water or unpurified bottled water. Our bodies do not want to swallow the toxins in water and regular tap water often has a "funny" taste. I've had mothers who struggled to get their children to drink water until they tried reverse osmosis purification. It becomes much easier for patients to drink half their body weight in water when the water is pure. You can truly taste the difference.

Getting Started

When I first became a patient of Dr. Pitman's, he told me that tap water could be harmful to my young children's immune system and recommended that I get a reverse osmosis (RO) system. I wasn't too worried because, at the time, it was practically impossible to get my children to drink water anyway.

Instead of investing in an RO system, I started bringing home gallons of RO water from the grocery store every week. When I began working on this book with Dr. Pitman, I learned about proper and improper storage and realized I was still contaminating our water.

I finally decided to invest in an RO system and discovered I could get a good system for $160 at the local hardware store. I had spent at least that amount over the last three months buying my water weekly, and besides, carrying gallons of water home was a huge hassle. I realized my resistance to look into the RO water earlier wasn't about money or time. It was simply a lack of commitment to becoming healthy.

Now that I have an RO system, I feel a bit healthier every time I turn on the faucet. Not only am I saving money by not having to buy my water, I'm also saving by not having to buy juice bags for my children. They love drinking the RO water. It tastes much better than tap water, and we have mostly eliminated unhealthy drinks from our household.

My children often request RO water over any other type of drink.

Here are the practicals: I have found on my journey to health that I don't always listen the first time, and it is usually because of money or time.

- *Once I make a firm commitment to one of the Ten Commandments of Ultimate Health — in this case, buying an RO system and drinking purified water—my family and I are healthier.*
- *I've discovered that I must invest the needed money, time, and energy — it is always worth it.*
- *When I do these things, I end up reaping benefits beyond what I could have imagined.*

THIRD COMMANDMENT:
SLEEP

"He grants sleep to those he loves." (Psalm 127:2)

"Come to me, all you who are weary and burdened, and I will give you rest." (Matthew 11:28)

"By the seventh day God had finished the work he had been doing; so on the seventh day he rested from all his work." (Genesis 2:2)

My wife and I were in my youngest son's room one evening, praying with him before he went to sleep. His phone lit up and vibrated to alert him that a text message had just been sent. He immediately became stimulated and jumped up to check his phone. He looked at the message and, as soon as he was comfortable again, the phone vibrated with another text message, jolting him from his relaxed state. We decided to remove the phone from his bedroom from that evening forward because we thought it was likely to disrupt his sleep — and he is not alone.

My older son is a manager of the basketball team at a major university. One of his jobs is to collect the cell phones the night before a big game, minimizing the chance that the players will be disturbed in the middle of the night.

The Pew Research Center notes that four out of five teens sleep with their phones; in fact, teens who use their cell phones to text are

42 percent more likely to sleep with their phones than teens who own phones but don't text. This lack of sleep can lead to sleep deprivation and has been associated with memory deficits, impaired performance, and reduced concentration and creativity.[15] Sleep deprivation puts adolescents at risk for cognitive and emotional difficulties and even accidents and psychopathology.[16]

> The Pew Research Center notes that four out of five teens sleep with their phones; in fact, teens who use their cell phones to text are 42 percent more likely to sleep with their phones than teens who own phones but don't text.

Teens are not alone in having technology disrupt their sleep. For years I have been aware that watching the 11 p.m. news can actually disturb our sleep patterns. Watching disturbing night news can raise our cortisol levels, lower our blood sugar, and trigger the autonomic nervous system to an awakened state. This physiological reaction mirrors our body's reaction to stress, and it is not good for us on a continual basis.

We not only have to turn off the lights to ensure a good night's sleep, but we have to turn off the computer, phone, television, iPad, and any other vibrating, light-shedding technological device. All of these things can be detrimental to a good night's sleep.

Sleep is essential to good health. The National Sleep Foundation warns that people with insomnia have 10 times the risk of developing depression compared with those who sleep well.[17] A 2010 Penn State study reported that insomniac men who slept less than six hours per day quadrupled their risk for early death.[18]

Sleep regulates your hormones and promotes the neurotransmitter balance in the brain, leading to less irritability and thus making people less prone to depression and anxiety. It also slows the aging process, boosts your immune system, and improves brain function.

Benjamin Franklin's old adage of "Early to bed and early to rise, makes a man healthy, wealthy, and wise" is still true. Vital sleep occurs between the hours of 10 p.m. and midnight. These are the hours in which physical healing takes place. Each hour of sleep that you get before midnight is equal to two hours of sleep after midnight. Sleep between the hours of midnight and 5 a.m. is psychological rest. Your body should rest seven to eight hours a night. Ideally, those hours would be from 9 or 10 p.m. to 5 a.m. Before the advent of electricity and the technology age, humans would rest from sundown to sunrise, and our bodies still benefit from following this age- old practice. If you are not asleep by 10 p.m., your body begins to feel hungry and looks for energy to stay awake (again, because cortisol levels are rising). Patients have reported weight loss or weight gain based on their sleep patterns.

Sleep patterns can be chronically disrupted when we begin to dismiss the sleep and awaken signals our body is sending out.[19] Being in bed before 10 p.m. is a gift to your body, allowing it to follow its natural rhythm. Proper sleep may be one of the ways we can decrease our risk of cancer. When you follow your natural circadian rhythm, your body develops proper levels of melatonin, a natural antioxidant.

Many patients ask me about sleeping on their back versus their sides. For optimal chiropractic health, sleeping on your back is best for alignment. If you sleep on your side, use a pillow that supports the spine. Sleeping on your stomach is not good for your health. Your neck and spine are twisted all night long, causing stress to the nervous system.

Ultimately, sleep is vital to being healthy. Follow these three steps for a healthier you:

1. Turn off all technological devices and artificial light for a sounder, uninterrupted sleep.
2. Live by the motto: "Early to bed, early to rise."
3. Sleep on your back or use a chiropractic pillow for side sleeping.

Getting Started

Who doesn't like sleep? For me, this is more of a luxury than a commandment.

When I first started seeing Dr. Pitman, I learned more about the importance of going to sleep by 10 p.m, nightly. I thought it would be hard to change my sleep schedule. Then one night around 9:30 p.m., I realized that my body really wanted to slow down. Dr. Pitman's advice gave me an "excuse" to go to bed early. I was amazed at how quickly my body adjusted to a 10 p.m. to 5 a.m. schedule, versus the midnight to 7 a.m. one.

I still get an hour or two to clean and accomplish something while my young children are sleeping, but this precious time is often in the morning now. I no longer fight going to sleep, and I listen to the signals my body is sending out. I don't feel as tired throughout the day as I used to. In my experience, this is one of the Commandments of Ultimate Health that has immediate results. After a good night's sleep, you feel better the next day.

The practicals? I'll repeat the three points Dr. Pitman just mentioned:
1. *Turn off all technological devices and artificial light for a sounder, uninterrupted sleep.*
2. *Live by the motto: "Early to bed, early to rise."*
3. *Sleep on your back or use a chiropractic pillow for side sleeping.*

FOURTH COMMANDMENT:
EAT CLEAN, LIVING FOODS

"The land produced vegetation: plants bearing seed according to their kinds, and trees bearing fruit with seed in it according to their kinds. . . . And God saw that it was good." (Genesis 1:12)

"Then God said, 'I give you every seed-bearing plant on the face of the whole earth and every tree that has fruit with seed in it.'"
(Genesis 1:29)

The king told his chief of staff to get some young men who were the brightest and most handsome and had the most potential to become the next generation of leaders. The king was going to train the men for three years and feed them directly from his table, allowing them to eat the same food and wine as the king himself.

Daniel and three friends were among those selected. However, Daniel decided that he would not defile himself by eating the king's food or drinking his wine, so he asked the head of staff if he could skip the royal diet. This staff person liked Daniel, but he was afraid that if Daniel and his friends appeared frail and weak, he would be beheaded because he didn't follow the king's orders. Eventually, the two struck a deal. Daniel and his three friends would abstain from the king's food and have a diet of vegetables and water. After a short test, the chief of staff could judge the appearance of Daniel and his friends and decide if they could continue the diet.

At the end of 10 days, Daniel and his friends looked better, more nourished, and healthier than their counterparts who were eating from the king's table. The chief allowed them to continue their diet. At the end of the training period, the king was more impressed with Daniel and his three friends than he was with any of the other men. God blessed Daniel and his friends with great knowledge, and they became the best and the brightest in the nation.

It may be even more difficult today than in Daniel's time (Daniel 1) to part with the ways of the world and eat clean, living foods. Clean food is food that does not have contaminants like preservatives, artificial flavorings, colorings, and pesticides. Living food is food that comes from the ground.

A patient of mine became frustrated when she realized that after trying to feed her children healthy food, the entire diet for one of her children had been blown in a single afternoon. She realized that after attending a birthday party, her child had eaten more than 178 grams of sugar (or 41.9 teaspoons)!

The American Heart Association recommends three teaspoons (12.8 grams) of sugar a day for children between the ages of four and eight.[21] Her child had taken in more than 14 times the recommended allowance in a single afternoon—approximately two weeks' worth of sugar. But sugar is only one of our worries. In that same afternoon, this same child had at least 18 preservatives and a minimum of four types of food dyes.

> **Even if all the sugar, dyes, and preservatives were eliminated, it is likely that the foods the child ate that day had little nutritional value.**

Even if all the sugar, dyes, and preservatives were eliminated, it is likely that the foods the child ate that day had little nutritional value. That's right; even before the bad stuff is added to our food, we often start off with a grain that has had basically all of the good stuff "gutted" out of it.

In the case of wheat, the germ and the bran are removed during processing to create white flour. The germ and the bran are the most nutritious components of the wheat. Without these nutrients, we are eating dead food, a substance that has had just about everything good ripped from it.

Why do we gut the good nutrients from our food? It increases shelf life. The good part of the food, the nutrients, are alive and are more prone to spoiling. According to Michael Pollan, author of *In Defense of Food*, the lack of nutrients actually makes the food less appealing to rodents.[22] Is it true that we are eating foods that would be a rat's second — or even farther down than that — choice?

My father-in-law is a farmer and produces thousands of bushels of corn per year. The best corn is purchased by those who make ethanol. The lowest-grade corn is what is used in processed food and is made into corn syrup. We use the lowest-grade corn, and then we process it into a substance that doesn't resemble corn at all.

> We are eating stripped-down, low-grade food that is placed in a box where it is covered with sugar, preservatives, and dyes and labeled with a creative slogan and strong marketing brand.

We are eating stripped-down, low-grade food that is placed in a box where it is covered with sugar, preservatives, and dyes and labeled with a creative slogan and strong marketing brand.

According to Nutrition Action, in 1971, a typical supermarket carried a little less than 8,000 items. In 2009, your average grocery store carries more than 48,000.[23] About 15 percent of this increase can be justified by imported foods, but the additional foods are simply varieties of creatively packaged dead foods.

According to the USDA, we are eating 500 more calories per day than we did in 1970. We have added extra calories while most people still do not eat the recommended amount of fruits and vegetables, tipping the scales even more toward dead food.[24]

We are inundated with more and more processed food-like substances every year that couldn't be further from the foods that Daniel ate. Like Daniel, we need to separate from the culture around us and make our best attempt to eat living foods. Living foods are harvested out of the ground. They are colorful and full of the nutrients we need to have energy.[25]

Today's children have a shorter life expectancy than their parents. One out of three children born in the year 2000 will develop diabetes — make that one in two if the child is black or Hispanic. Obesity rates among children have doubled in the last 10 years and tripled for adolescents.[26] According to the American Public Health Association, 15 percent of U.S. children are overweight and an additional 15 percent at risk of becoming overweight.[27]

High fructose corn syrup is often blamed for the obesity epidemic — and rightly so. High fructose corn syrup is genetically altered corn syrup; it is designed to make the taste even sweeter than sugar. Since it is genetically altered, it doesn't do what a real sweetener does. It doesn't inform our brains that we are full.[28]

You also need to be educated about foods that have aspartame and Splenda in them. The February 2011 Health Alert links aspartame, the sweetener in most diet sodas, to multiple sclerosis, systemic lupus, fibromyalgia, neuropathy, seizures, chronic fatigue, and stealth disease (autoimmune diseases that invade the body's tissue).[29] Splenda contains chlorine.[30]

Dead foods lead to obesity because, even though we are eating, we are malnourished. We are malnourished, overweight people, left feeling hungry and with little energy. Foods packaged for particular diets are often packed with artificial sweeteners. They are not only dead foods that do not provide your body with nutrients, they may be toxic to some individuals.

According to the Center for Science in the Public Interest, in 2008 McDonald's spent $1.2 billion on advertising, and total domestic food, beverage, and restaurant advertising has reached

11 billion dollars. For every dollar spent in advertising that tells us the benefits of eating fruits and vegetables, the food and beverage industry spends $1,100.[31]

Many patients ask about eating meat. Our genetic code is designed according to our nationality. Most of us in the United States are, we could say, genetic mutts, and thus we require more protein than an individual whose genetic code is 100 percent Asian. Protein can be plant- or vegetable-based. Although meat is not "living," it can be incorporated into a healthy diet if it is farm-raised and organic. I ask my patients to shoot for a diet that is approximately 70 percent living food. Meat would count toward the 30 percent of dead foods being eaten.

> It is time to be like Daniel and stand apart from those around us, even when the messages that surround us encourage us to consume more and more dead foods.

Finally, when eating foods that do come from the ground, purchase organic foods whenever possible. I have included extensive information about pesticides in morbific stimuli in the second half of this book.

It is time to be like Daniel and stand apart from those around us, even when the messages that surround us encourage us to consume more and more dead foods. Here are the tips you need to get started:

1. Shop the perimeter of the grocery store. Dead foods are found in the middle aisles on shelves. Your living foods—produce, fresh fish, and eggs—can typically be found in the outer boundaries of the store.

2. Become a label reader. Look for foods that have three to six ingredients in them and beware of ingredients that sound like chemicals.

3. Buy foods from local farmers and at farmers markets. Visit their farms. Be able to shake hands with the people who grow

your foods. Know where and how your meat is raised.

4. Buy clean, organic foods as much as possible, and make sure to use a quality spray that removes pesticides when organics are not available.

5. Work toward having 70 percent of your foods as living – foods that are harvested from the ground and are not packaged.

Getting Started

Eating clean isn't easy. How did the biblical Daniel do it? Every morning, I wonder . . . What did Daniel eat for breakfast? Am I supposed to gnaw on some cabbage instead of pouring processed cereal into a bowl? Then I think, Well, Daniel didn't have kids, did he? I try to strike the balance and prepare a high-quality protein shake for myself and my children. I am not sure if Daniel or Dr. Pitman would approve, but I feel better knowing that I have traded dead foods for some amino acids and vitamins.

Improving my diet has been a process. I have taken baby steps toward improving my family's eating habits. Even though it is not perfect, I know our diet is significantly improved. Here's how I started:

- *Buy organic: The first thing I did was buy organic produce whenever possible. It may be more expensive in the grocery store, but if you skip the fruit snacks, you have an extra dollar to afford the berries. Farmers markets are a great resource for things like organic, free range eggs and local, seasonal produce.*

- *Avoid processed foods: I tried this, but discovered that as a busy, working mom, I couldn't avoid them all. I began to read labels. You can buy a bag of chips that has 30 ingredients, many of which you can't pronounce, or you can buy a bag with three ingredients— potatoes, oil, and salt. The price is the same. It just takes a few extra moments to discover which package contains food and which package contains chemicals.*

- *Good friends keep each other healthy: I have a network of friends that also buys organic. We share coupons and call each other when we see a sale or hard-to-find organic products. I have been amazed to find this support network during this short, three-year period. Talking about your efforts to buy organic foods will connect you with other like-minded individuals. When you work together, you save time, energy, and dollars while building friendships along the way.*

- *Cook right: I actually cook less on a nightly basis. I can easily prepare a protein source and combine it with lots of raw vegetables for a quick dinner. I avoid cooking packaged starches or casseroles. It is simple, but it works. Recently I started roasting vegetables every Sunday and placing them in a large container to use throughout the week. It has helped me to include a wider variety of vegetables —squash, beets, zucchini, and peppers — into our diet. Not only does this make me feel more like Daniel, they taste so good that I feel like a gourmet cook!*

On a biweekly or monthly basis, I cook cakes, breads, or other treats from scratch. I discovered that making pancakes from scratch, instead of from a box, takes about two extra minutes, and I can ensure that the products are organic. I can also incorporate things like whole grain flour, flax, and whole organic cornmeal in my cooking whenever possible.

- *Go for farm-raised beef: I also purchased a freezer and bought a quarter of a cow from a local farmer. You can actually visit the farm and the processor to make sure you are getting top-quality meat. Look for qualities such as the animal being grass-fed, having little to no antibiotics, eating organic food, and not being raised in a factory. You will likely get a higher quality product that is economical. Having quality meat in your freezer is also a convenience.*

Even after all of these efforts, I'm still not eating like Daniel. I'm constantly making efforts to incorporate more salads and greens into my family's diet. I also find that high-quality, "clean" protein shakes and organic raw food bars can make a tremendous difference on busy days.

I hope, some day, to make it to a consistent, clean diet, following the

"70 percent clean" rule. Until that day, I will continue to rely on my support network and read this book for encouragement. I know it will come.

FIFTH COMMANDMENT:
USE CHIROPRACTIC CARE

"His father was sick in bed, suffering from fever and dysentery. Paul went in to see him and, after prayer, placed his hands on him and healed him." (Acts 28:8)

"He could not do any miracles there, except lay his hands on a few sick people and heal them." (Mark 6:5)

"Then he put his hands on her, and immediately she straightened up and praised God." (Luke 13:13).

Although manipulation has been used for thousands of years and practiced around the world, no one knows for sure what happened before, during, or after the first modern chiropractic adjustment, in 1895.

There are different accounts from relatives and friends, and although some documentation is available, we can't be sure why the first chiropractic patient, Harvey Lillard, trusted D.D. Palmer, the father of chiropractic, to adjust his back. Even less is known about the second and third and 50th chiropractic patients, but we do know that they were pioneers, creating a science for more than 50,000 chiropractors and their patients today.

Like Harvey Lillard did in visiting Palmer, many patients today have exhausted other options before coming to my office. Lillard had been partially deaf for 17 years. He had this hearing loss not because something was wrong with his ears, but because there was a misalignment in his back. Chiropractic care treats *the cause* of your symptoms instead of just treating the symptoms alone. Chiropractic care removes interferences within the body.

Every decision made in the body starts in the brain and travels down the spinal cord to the peripheral nervous system. The peripheral nervous system is comprised of all the rest of the nerves in the body. When you touch a hot stove, the peripheral nervous system sends a message to the brain. The brain registers that it is hot and sends the message back down the peripheral nervous system for you to remove your hand. What would happen if the peripheral nervous system was blocked?

Take a quick quiz. If you had a rock sitting on your foot, you should:

A. Take some ibuprofen for your foot.

B. Remove your foot surgically.

C. Remove the rock.

The correct answer is clearly C: remove the rock. Yet when it comes to medical care, we are much quicker to take some medicine or go to more drastic measures to resolve the symptoms of our problems. Chiropractic removes the block, the source of the problem, instead of covering it up. These blockages of the spine are called *subluxations*. If a vertebra becomes misaligned, it can cause irritation, inflammation, pain, and malfunction. Removal of these subluxations and interferences restores the body to a more balanced state of health.

There is a myth that once you go to a chiropractor, you will have to continue to go back. The truth is, once you go to a chiropractor, you will want to go back because you will feel better and your body will function better. Continued chiropractic care allows the tissues around the bones to heal once an alignment has been corrected. Monthly adjustments keep the body aligned and functioning in a preventive mode, much like routine dental exams. By scheduling routine maintenance treatments, you can avoid unnecessary and expensive medications, tests, and surgeries. You will save significant dollars in the long run.

We do not live in a glass bubble. Our bodies are continually going through stress and trauma. Routine chiropractic care helps the body handle stress better.

After church one morning, I received a call from the son of a good friend. He told me that his father had been hospitalized because he had stroke-like symptoms. He was unable to move his left side or get out of bed. They decided that it had not been a stroke and were beginning to do neurological testing. Because of the severity of his situation, they were also making arrangements to move him from a neighborhood hospital to the University of Cincinnati. He had already been in the hospital for three days.

> We do not live in a glass bubble. Our bodies are continually going through stress and trauma. Routine chiropractic care helps the body handle stress better.

When I arrived, my friend still was not able to stand, as his entire left side was not functioning. I adjusted his neck and back, and within 20 minutes he was not only up and out of bed, he was packing up his things to leave the hospital.

This was the second time I had to make a hospital visit for this friend. The first time he presented different symptoms, but both times he was simply in need of a chiropractic adjustment. I told him on the way out the door, "This is your second and last hospital visit. You need to come in for regular adjustments to avoid this in the future." Think of all the time and money that a simple monthly adjustment would have saved my friend.

Since the days of Harvey Lillard, chiropractic care has become much more accepted into the mainstream of medical practices. It is covered by many insurance companies; however, it is important to remember that chiropractic care should be part of a health regimen that includes the other Ten Commandments of Ultimate Health.

Whenever I go to a chiropractic convention, I make it a habit to find the oldest chiropractor in the room, sit next to him, and befriend him. They almost always have wisdom and experience that I can benefit from. At a recent convention, a 79-year-old chiropractor made an observation that he is finding that his patients' bodies are so toxic that they are not holding the adjustments as well as they did a few decades ago. He said, "Because of the layers of toxicity, you just don't see the miracles as often as you used to."

I believe that God still wants us to experience the "healing miracles" from chiropractic care, and we will see them much more often when we combine chiropractic care with the other Commandments of Ultimate Health, reducing our toxicity and allowing our bodies to heal.

* * * * *

ANGELIA'S STORY

Our happy little baby girl suffered from chronic ear infections from just after her first birthday until she was two. At that time, the pediatrician wanted to put in ear tubes, but I just wasn't ready to have my child go through surgery.

Luckily, a friend recommended I take her to Dr. Pitman. He immediately surmised that she did not have a bacterial infection, but that she did have a fungal infection from all the antibiotics she had been given.

To make the situation worse, the bones around her head and ear were compressed. Dr. Pitman deducted that this occurred when she was pulled out of the birth canal using forceps. After her first chiropractic adjustment her ear infection went away—permanently!

The visit to Dr. Pitman changed our family's lives!

*— **Angelia Betscher, Amelia, Ohio***

RANDY'S TESTIMONY

I was playing golf one Sunday and developed severe pain up my arm to my shoulder. I was so sore that I couldn't even rotate the knob on Dr. Pitman's door. If I would have gone to a conventional doctor or physical therapy, it probably would have taken weeks to find relief. After an adjustment with Dr Pitman, I was immediately relieved of the pain, and it never came back. I could rotate the handle on the door on the way out with no problem.

— Randy Bernard, Cincinnati, Ohio

Getting Started

Since coming to Dr. Pitman, my husband, my two sons, and myself have experienced healing from his chiropractic techniques. The most memorable healing occurred with my oldest son, Noah.

My husband and I were spending thousands of dollars on speech and occupational therapy treatments on Noah. He had many issues including auditory processing and visual and sensory problems. We were already seeing Dr. Pitman for allergy treatments. I told him that his allergies were improving but his auditory processing issues were still there. "Has he ever had a chiropractic adjustment?" he asked. I agreed to have him adjusted.

The next time I saw his preschool teacher, she stopped me at her door. She knew I was trying some different therapies. "I don't know what you did, but he has improved since last week," she said. "It is a significant difference."

Our speech and occupational therapists noticed significant improvements, and we were able to discontinue their services. I made a commitment to have all of us adjusted on a monthly basis.

A few months into this, Noah's vision therapist suffered a significant illness and sold his practice. Without the vision therapy, Noah's vision was becoming worse, and his left eye didn't seem to be tracking or moving at all. We found a new eye doctor, and I mentioned my concern to Dr.

Pitman at one of our monthly appointments. Not only did Dr. Pitman adjust his neck, he also adjusted his eye. It was amazing. That same evening, my husband and I started to notice that his eye was tracking appropriately. Within that same month, he had significant athletic improvements, and his next eye exam was significantly improved.

Now Noah excels academically, socially, and in many other ways. He is no longer limited by the sensory issues that plagued him early on.

I've been amazed at the wide variety of things that chiropractic care can help. Dr. Pitman always encourages me to share the wide range of symptoms we have with him. I recommend:

- *Share a wide range of symptoms with your doctor — and make a commitment to use chiropractic care regularly.*
- *Combine chiropractic care with all the other Ten Commandments of Ultimate Health.*

SIXTH COMMANDMENT:
EXERCISE

"Do you not know that in a race all the runners run, but only one gets the prize? Run in such a way as to get the prize."
(1 Corinthians 9:24)

"For physical training is of some value, but godliness has value for all things, holding promise for both the present life and the life to come." (1 Timothy 4:8)

"And let us run with perseverance the race marked out for us."
(Hebrews 12:1)

By now, everyone in mainstream America knows that exercise is important for cardiovascular health and weight management. There is so much information on exercise that I could write an entire book (or two) about exercise alone. For now, I am going to concentrate on some key points.

Detoxification: Exercise detoxifies your body. Toxins are released through our sweat. Embrace the sweat and realize that it is your body letting go of harmful substances. Exercise also helps every organ system, increases bowel function, and increases oxygen to your cells. As your body works more efficiently, it will unload toxins more easily.

Brain Function: Exercise also improves brain function. When you exercise, you're sending messages to your brain to reconnect to a certain muscle group. This excites the brain function, sending positive signals back and forth between the muscles and the brain.

Exercise should cross the midline. If you drew a line both vertically and horizontally on your body, midline exercises would cross one of those lines. For example, touching the left hand to the right foot, and vice versa, or touching the right elbow to the left knee, or vice versa, are all "crossing midline" exercises. They increase communication between the two sides of the brain and the body. Most of the research about crossing the midline surrounds children, but the Journal of Gerontology reports that midline-crossing inhibitions on the lower extremities reemerge in individuals 65 years and older, giving an indication that midline exercises could be beneficial throughout life.[32] I have seen plenty of patients in their adulthood benefit from midline exercises, and we should all incorporate them into our exercise regimen for a better quality of life today as well as into our senior years.

Cardiovascular exercise: Walking, cycling, swimming, and using the elliptical machine are all ways to get your heart pumping and improve cardiovascular health. Intensity is important, so make sure you are sweating. A 1995, the Journal of American Medicine reported that vigorous activities, versus activities that were not vigorous, were associated with living longer in men.[33] The Journal of the American College of Nutrition noted that high-intensity exercise training without dietary manipulation resulted in a decrease in body fat.[34]

Isotonic exercise: Weight lifting or working with resistant bands is an example of isotonic exercise. This type of exercise is important because it slows the aging process and keeps our muscles strong for everyday use. The American College of Sports Medicine (ACSM) and the American Heart Association (AHA) released guidelines suggesting eight to ten strength-training exercises that work the chest, shoulders, arms, back, abdomen, and legs.[35]

Enjoy it! What is the best exercise? It depends on the person. Choose an exercise regimen that you enjoy. It should be fun . . . something that you can do daily. It takes three weeks for anything to become a habit; therefore, if you enjoy what you are doing, you are more likely to stick with it. Incorporate exercises that you can do winter, summer, spring, or fall, so you don't lose the habit at the change of a season.

Train for life: Most of us are training to keep our bodies healthy (not for the Olympics or the Ironman). Avoid excessive, repetitive movements for a long period of time that can cause injury. Exercising in the elderly years is important too, so consider swimming, the elliptical machine, Yoga, Pilates, biking, or the Cellerciser (discussed below) over activities that are hard on your body. These things will help preserve our bodies for the years to come.

> What is the best exercise? It depends on the person. Choose an exercise regimen that you enjoy. It should be fun . . . something that you can do daily.

Cellerciser: My favorite exercise is the Cellerciser®. It looks like a mini-rebounder or a mini-trampoline and it utilizes your body weight negatively and positively as you bounce.

By stabilizing various parts of your body for a minute or less, you can exercise every part of your body in as little as 10 minutes. When compared with a gym membership or a treadmill, the Cellerciser is an inexpensive exercise tool that works efficiently, giving an effective workout in a quick period of time.

I warn my patients that the Cellerciser can't be replaced with cheaper trampolines that aren't made with its triple-tiered springs that ensure a safer workout and help prevent foot and back injuries.

The Cellerciser improves posture, tone, and muscle function and enables 75 trillion cells to detoxify in a single 10-minute workout. The Cellerciser is an extremely efficient workout, inexpensive, appropriate for all ages, and can be used winter, summer, spring, or fall. It provides an intense cardio workout as well as isotonic training. By stabilizing your muscles as you bounce, it creates the same effect as if you are lifting weights. It's also an easy way to incorporate midline exercises, connecting your brain and body through movement.[36]

For more information on the Cellerciser, see www.cellerciser.com. It really is an amazing exercise that increases detoxification while incorporating cardio, weight resistance, and midline brain movements into one enjoyable, quick workout.

I always think of the late chiropractor and bodybuilder Jack LaLanne (see his exercises and more information about him at www.jacklalanne.com). He was the Godfather of Fitness and had the first television fitness show. He always marveled at the body that God gave us and asked his viewers to take care of their bodies, that those bodies were presents from God. By exercising and eating right, we are showing gratitude for our bodies. LaLanne also asked viewers to look at themselves for what they can be, not necessarily for what they are today.[37]

> He always marveled at the body that God gave us and asked his viewers to take care of their bodies, that those bodies were presents from God. By exercising and eating right, we are showing gratitude for our bodies.

Whether you use Jack LaLanne's simple but effective exercises, the Cellerciser, or another activity of choice, exercise and the Ten Commandments of Ultimate Health can lead you to new, exciting places. As Lalaane said, "Anything in life is possible, and you can make it happen."[38]

Getting Started

The greatest part about the Cellerciser is that it is a great way to get started for people, like me, who were, or are, out of shape and obese. Only having to do it for 10 minutes is a great gift. It can be accomplished in the privacy of your own home, which can help the out-of-shape, overweight person who might feel self-conscious in a gym.

After doing the Cellerciser and walking with a friend for several months, I included running, weight lifting with a personal trainer, and a cross-fit class into my exercise regimen. I discovered that my favorite exercise is any exercise that I do with another person. With raising children, I can't afford or schedule in group exercise every day, so I still rely on my Cellerciser to keep me moving when I can't join others for a workout.

I still may not look like a model, but my BMI (body mass index) has improved significantly, moving down six points. If I use Jack LaLanne's philosophy of looking at myself not as I am today, but for who I can be . . . the future is bright!

The practicals, as simple as I can make them:

- Just get started! Whether the Cellerciser or walking or running or Isotonic or cross-fit — get started. And have fun!

- Enlist a friend. It's easier to exercise with a friend. Again, my favorite exercise is any exercising I do with a friend.

SEVENTH COMMANDMENT:
PURIFICATION

"If you return to the Almighty, you will be restored." (Job 22:23)

*"Look on me and answer, Lord my God. Give light to my eyes, or
I will sleep in death."* (Psalm 13:3)

*"Jesus, full of the Holy Spirit, left the Jordan and was led by the
Spirit into the wilderness, where for forty days he was tempted
by the devil. He ate nothing during those days, and at the end of
them he was hungry."* (Luke 4:1, 2)

God is forgiving. He forgives the repentant for their
sins . . . no matter what the sin is. As a Christian, I take
comfort in knowing that my soul can be cleansed. We can
also take comfort in knowing that, here on earth, our bodies can be
cleansed.

So often, individuals don't begin to take the needed steps toward
a healthier lifestyle because they believe it's too late. They have been a
smoker, eaten poorly, drank too much, haven't exercised — or some
combination, or all of those things — and feel the damage has been
done.

I've had patients who asked me, "Can I really get all the bad stuff
I have put in my body out of my body?" I tell them that their cells
are constantly changing, and every cell in their body will be replaced
in seven years. In that relatively short amount of time, they will have

a completely new and different body. What they do today is actually creating a blueprint for their future cells. We can start to change our cells positively by following the Ten Commandments of Ultimate Health and releasing toxins through purification. We can bring our bodies back to homeostasis and can make our blood cells and bone cells totally new.

Almost everyone needs to go through a purification process. Can you imagine driving a car for 10 years without changing the filter? Cleansing is like changing the filter of your body. This filter gives your organs an opportunity to release toxins.

Purification helps you remove the toxins that occur in daily living. It can also help you maintain a healthy weight. Some examples of toxins are: air and water pollutants, caffeine, cigarette smoke, cosmetics, heavy metals, household cleaning products, pesticides and herbicides, pharmaceuticals, and preservatives.[39] There are more than 80,000 synthetic chemicals registered for use in the United States.[40] Many of these chemicals are present in your body. These synthetic chemicals disrupt our immune, endocrine, and reproductive systems.[41]

> There are more than 80,000 synthetic chemicals registered for use in the United States. Many of these chemicals are present in your body.

Here is a test to determine if you can benefit from a detoxification process.

1. Do you eat foods that are packaged or processed?
2. Do you eat meat or poultry that is not antibiotic-free, free range, and organic?
3. Do you eat produce that is not organic?
4. Do you or have you overloaded your liver with sugar or artificial sweeteners?
5. Do you drink soda pop?
6. Do you eat foods that have artificial colors, preservatives, or

additives?

7. Do you eat out often?

8. Do you drink alcohol?

9. Do you drink water that is not filtered through a reverse osmosis system?

If you answered yes to any of the above, you could benefit from a purification process.

There are many ways to purify the body.

When you exercise and really sweat, you are cleansing your body. Taking supplements and even certain types of herbal baths help to rid your body of toxins. Following many of the Ten Commandments of Ultimate Health, drinking water, eating clean/living foods, exercising, and supplementation can help your body cleanse.

Chewing your food helps with digestion. When you chew your food, enzymes are secreted in your mouth that aid the digestion process. When you predigest the food in your mouth, it puts less stress on the digestive process. I always tell the kids in my practice to "Chew! Chew! Chew! When you eat, think of a train saying 'Choo! Choo! Choo!'"

I recommend a 21-day program to help cleanse the body of all the "bad stuff," and a 40-day "clean food diet" to create a habit. Most purification plans include eating mostly vegetables, oil, fruit, and lentils and drinking reverse osmosis or distilled water. Others include supplementation that provides a daily cleanse. Purification can lead to improved weight management, increased energy, and the disappearance of past conditions.

See our website, www.familytreecc.com for more ideas about cleansing and purifying your system.

Getting Started

This is, for me, the most difficult health commandment. I have successfully cleansed only once since I met Dr. Pitman. I started by drinking a cleanse shake and eating mainly vegetables and a little bit of fruit. A few times, I incorporated a cup of rice or a few ounces of naturally raised chicken. I think I was able to do it only because I was working on this book extensively at the time and was constantly reminded about the importance of my health.

My suggestion is to stock up on fresh produce, a high quality cleanse shake, and keep the book in hand to remind you of the importance of cleansing.

Cleansing will help you gain back what I call your "food sanity."

I have only had this type of sanity for a few days of my life. After cleansing for more than a week, I had the most unusual experience. I was helping a friend clean up after a Super Bowl party and looked down at someone else's plate. I saw chicken wings smothered in dark, sugary, barbecue sauce, processed and artificially colored chips, and artificially colored candies. I suddenly felt like I was going to vomit. I ran to the bathroom. In that moment, I saw these fake food substances for what they really are, chemical toxins that are made to look like foods. I believe the vomit was my body's visceral reaction. I had gained back my food sanity. In that one moment, I was able to recognize what was food and what was toxic. It was a great gift.

In this world, I think it is difficult to maintain food sanity. I know that I haven't been able to do it, so I guess another cleanse is in order.

- *Determine that you are going to cleanse. Use the ideas in this chapter, and go to www.familytreecc.com for more ideas.*
- *Stock up on fresh produce, a high quality cleanse shake, and keep this book in hand to remind you of the importance of cleansing.*

EIGHTH COMMANDMENT:
TAKE NUTRITIONAL SUPPLEMENTS

"Then their father Israel said to them, 'If it must be, then do this: Put some of the best products of the land in your bags and take them down to the man as a gift — a little balm and a little honey, some spices and myrrh, some pistachio nuts and almonds.'"
(Genesis 43:11)

"On coming to the house, they saw the child with his mother Mary, and they bowed down and worshiped him. Then they opened their treasures and presented him with gifts of gold, frankincense and myrrh." (Matthew 2:11)

Many people believe the myth that if you eat right, you do not need to take supplements. But who truly eats right? To say that you are eating right would mean that your diet is balanced and free of hormones, soda, artificial sweeteners, white sugar, processed foods, nonorganic foods, alcohol, and food cooked in most restaurants.

Supplements promote purification via detoxification. They increase cell function, improve ATP synthesis (energy production in the cell), and facilitate the healing process. Most diseases are caused by a nutritional deficiency. The right supplements for a person can help to avoid these deficiencies.[42]

All supplements are not the same. Typically, synthetic vitamins are very inexpensive; however, they are not as effective. These less expensive vitamins may not properly dissolve during digestion, preventing the body from utilizing any of the good nutrients they would otherwise offer.

An independent consumer organization, Consumerlab.com, discovered that 13 out of 38 multivitamins were improperly labeled.[43] I recommend using vitamins and herbs from well-respected companies. For a complete list of recommended suppliers, see my website at www.familytreecc.com.

> There is truly only one way to make it through the maze of supplements out there in order to get what your body needs: Autonomic Reflex Testing.

In 2002, the American Medical Association shocked the medical community by publishing a study that recommended that all adults take a multivitamin supplement to prevent chronic disease.[44] In recent years, however, there have been many controversial studies that indicate that multivitamins may not be beneficial, and too many of them may actually be harmful to your health.

Even with negative information and research coming to the forefront on vitamins, 37 percent of us take vitamins daily. I think people continue to take supplements because they feel better or know someone who feels better because they take vitamins. I also believe that research on vitamins is challenging because every individual has unique needs, different deficiencies, and a one-of-kind genetic makeup. I have treated thousands of patients and it would be difficult for me to find two patients that need the same exact vitamins.

There is truly only one way to make it through the maze of supplements out there in order to get what your body needs: Autonomic Reflex Testing, or, as it is more commonly called, muscle testing. An autonomic nervous system response determines whether something is right or wrong for your body.

Autonomic Reflex Testing looks like this: while you are holding a nutritional supplement, a skilled practitioner attempts to push your arm down. If you are weaker while holding the substance than without it, the substance is wrong for your body. If you are stronger while holding the substance, the substance is OK for you.

Let's get scientific: A neuro-physiological response is stimulated during Autonomic Reflex Testing. This information runs down the ascending fibers along the spinothalamic track into the dorsal horn and the ascending fibers into the memory part of the brain. The brain calculates the information and sends a response down the spinal chord on ascending tracks to the anterior horn cells, giving a response.

Autonomic Reflex Testing has saved lives in my practice. It has helped to pinpoint substances that children were allergic to that other medical testing could not uncover. It has identified the right supplements to treat viruses and bacteria infections spiraling out of control. It has helped children recover from ADHD, autism, and asthma as well as adults suffering from fibromyalgia, allergies, and even cancer.

The Bible says that your body is the temple of the Holy Spirit. It was beautifully made by God. Autonomic Reflex Testing is one of the ways that you can rely on it to give you the answers you need, and it is through this nutritional testing that proper supplementation for each individual can be identified.

EMILY'S STORY

Emily had a horrendous history of painful kidney stones. In the spring of her seventh-grade year, she began experiencing the blinding pain of kidney stones once again. Emily did have another kidney stone, but the doctor's diagnosis was that the stone was too small to cause the pain Emily felt. Despite desperate attempts by her parents to probe further and find a solution for their daughter's pain, the doctor dismissed their concerns.

Over the summer of her eighth-grade year, Emily lost 14 pounds, bringing her weight to a ghastly 92 pounds. Her parents were constantly advocating for her with the urologist, and now an eating disorder specialist, but the pain was worsening. The once vibrant child was vacant and pale.

She missed her first day of eighth grade because she was hospitalized and put on a morphine pump. Even the morphine could not free her from the pain. The doctors were growing increasingly dismissive. Her parents were demanding treatment and answers. All that was given was pain management.

Finally, in October, surgery was performed to remove the same small stone that was now lodged in her ureter. After the surgery, the complications were intense. Emily's cries were so violent that she was given oxygen. Eventually the source of the pain was found. Emily's ureter had swelled around the catheter and was causing blinding pain.

The holidays came and went and, by February, Emily had a new problem, constipation. Emily was referred to a gastroenterologist. Emily was constipated for nine days, then for 14. The prescription was Miralax and more laxatives.

Eventually, in March, an ultrasound revealed that her kidneys were swollen. Medical X-rays showed that the stool inside her had backed all the way up her intestines. Emily was hospitalized and put on intense laxatives that were supposed to clean her out in 24 hours. They didn't start to work for three days.

Her parents were growing frustrated with the unending doctor bills, hospitalizations, and procedures. Where was the game plan? How could they free Emily from this pain? Would she ever be able to live a normal childhood life again? Whatever respect they had for the medical community was gone. The doctors could not see past their specialties long enough to confer with the other specialists.

By now, Emily's journey was well known to many people. She was on many prayer lists. At her brother's baseball game, her parents met Dr. Pitman. Dr. Pitman met with Emily the next week. His first test was a saliva test that denotes the age of your body. Emily was a 14-year-old girl . . . with the saliva of an 86-year-old.

Dr. Pitman treated the whole Emily, not just her kidney or her bowels. He talked to her, not her parents. Dr. Pitman slowly gained Emily's trust as he confirmed, through his treatments, how she was feeling. After Emily's first adjustment, she was not constipated again.

> Her parents were growing frustrated with the unending doctor bills, hospitalizations, and procedures. Where was the game plan?

Emily went to Dr. Pitman's office three times a week for the first three months. She had nutritional testing done that revealed her adrenal glands were barely functioning. Emily was very diligent and took all the prescribed supplements and homeopathic remedies.

As Emily progressed through the treatments, the old Emily started to reemerge. She was no longer hunched over and withdrawn. Her vibrant personality and coloring returned. After one year at Dr. Pitman's office, Emily was a healthy 105 pounds.

Emily's parents attribute her success with Dr. Pitman because he honored who she was as a person and approached her as a whole person, not a bunch of separate parts. The combinations of chiropractic care and supplementation were able to heal Emily completely, allowing her to be a healthy, thriving child.

* * * * *

FRANK'S TESTIMONY

In the spring of 1995 I was diagnosed with severe congestive heart disease.

My recuperation was good for several years, except that, once in a while, my doctor would have to adjust my medication if a slightly negative change was noted on my EKG.

I had regular checkups and usually, with whatever changes in prescriptions the doctor made, I felt blessed to be kept at a stage of health in which I could work and lead a social life with my children and grandchildren. Things remained about the same for some time.

During the past two and a half years, however, I have also been under the care of Dr. Greg Pitman of the Family Tree Chiropractic office. He suggested that I take a cardiac supplement regimen. After having my most recent regular checkup, the cardiologist called my home to report that my tests were good. "In fact, a little better," he said. This was good news, and on my next visit he actually cut the dosage of my digoxin (used to treat congestive heart failure) in half.

This improvement can only be attributed to adding my supplement regime, since the cardiologist made no other changes during the time I saw Dr. Pitman.

— **Frank T., Delhi, Ohio**

Getting Started

I always believed that supplements had value, but I thought they were less effective than modern medicines. I changed my mind about supplements a few months after sending my boys to Dr. Pitman. My youngest son, Nathan, had a chronic cough, and it was getting worse. The tight- sounding cough chilled my spine, as I had heard it numerous times before. It was winter, and Nathan, age two, had reoccurring bouts with pneumonia. He had been on a string of antibiotics. Within days of finishing his antibiotics, his cough would typically resurface.

Dr. Pitman suggested I use myrrh. I remember asking him: "What are you . . . a wise man?" I was making a biblical reference to the three kings. I laughed; the thought of being asked to give my child myrrh seemed odd. I expected him to give me Vitamin C, garlic, or zinc . . . but not myrrh. I remembered that I was taught that myrrh was given to Jesus because it had medicinal purposes, so I decided to try it.

Considering the cough was becoming severe, Dr. Pitman told me to give Nathan myrrh every hour. At first, the myrrh seemed to worsen the cough. My sister, a nurse, encouraged me to continue with the myrrh, reminding me that conventional medicine hadn't cured this cough in more than a year. "I am not sure what choice you have. This is the only thing you haven't tried," she said. "Give it another few hours."

Nathan and I were up in the wee hours of the night, trying to manage his cough by keeping him in an upright position. I took him downstairs for another round of myrrh when he started projectile vomiting across the kitchen floor. My first instinct was that the myrrh was making him sick, but after a few moments, I realized he was vomiting mucus. For over 20 minutes, Nathan jerked and cried as mucus violently erupted from his tiny body.

Once I realized what was happening, I became joyful. I realized that this mucus that had been causing havoc in his tiny body was finally coming out. I literally sang in praise as I knew this was a healing—a disgusting one, but a healing nonetheless.

My entire kitchen floor was covered in mucus. After using all of my kitchen towels, I had to get a bath towel to finish the cleanup. How could this much mucus be inside a two-year-old?

I began to understand that supplements address the cause, not just symptoms.

Since this time, we have used supplements successfully to treat viruses, bacterial infections, parasites, aches and pains, and much more. I am medication-free.

I believe that supplements would have a better reputation in the mainstream if we all had access to a qualified professional like Dr. Pitman.

Just one practical to close this chapter:

• Find a homeopath with a good reputation instead of browsing through the grocery store aisle on your own. It makes all the difference.

NINTH COMMANDMENT:
COPE WITH STRESS

"You will keep in perfect peace him whose mind is steadfast, because they trust in you." (Isaiah 26:3)

"Trouble and distress have come upon me, but your commands give me delight." (Psalm 119:143)

"My God is my rock, in whom I take refuge, my shield and the horn of my salvation. He is my stronghold, my refuge and my savior; from violent men you save me." (2 Samuel 22:3)

Managing the work-life balance, plummeting real estate values, running late, bills to pay, too little time, presentations, college tuition, and raising teenagers . . . all of these things cause stress in my life.

What's on your list?

There is no avoiding it. Stress is everywhere. There is good stress and bad stress, but stress has to be managed.

According to Nutrition Action, people are as much as five times more likely to develop colds if they are experiencing significant stress in their lives, such as unemployment, marital problems, or conflicts with friends.[45]

Stress can have a long-term impact if it is not dealt with. It is stored in the deep limbic system of the body called the hippocampus. Your body remembers the bad stress it has endured in the past.[46]

Stress causes your body to decrease the neurotransmitter serotonin and increase its cortisol, a steroid hormone. It can reduce your blood insulin levels and cause blood sugar issues. Stress also increases cholesterol and blood pressure. Stress increases anxiety and can lead to depression, anger — even memory loss.[47]

The list of ailments attributed to stress seems endless. What doesn't stress do? It doesn't go away, so we must have strategies for dealing with it.

> The list of ailments attributed to stress seems endless. What doesn't stress do? It doesn't go away, so we must have strategies for dealing with it.

I have five strategies for dealing with stress that I use, and I believe they have helped my patients as well.

Pray: Pray and remember that everything happens in God's timing, not our timing. I try to look through the eyes of Jesus and remember that there are reasons for things that I can't see. I am reminded of Thessalonians 5:16, 17: "Rejoice always; pray continually." Hebrews 13:5, 6 promises: "Never will I leave you, never will I forsake you. So we say with confidence, 'The Lord is my helper; I will not be afraid.'"

A Change Will Do You Good: Often I can choose to change my actions or my attitude. I have to realize that I can only change myself. It helps me to take ownership of the situations in my life.

Forgiveness: Letting go of guilt, fear, and shame. Asking God for forgiveness and forgiving myself can be difficult, but it eliminates the stressful burden of carrying around negative feelings.

Follow the Ten Commandments of Ultimate Health: These commandments provide a discipline that guides me through stressful periods. Prayer, exercise, and sleep are consistently shown to reduce stress, and others commandments, such as eating living foods, chiropractic care, and taking nutritional supplements will support you through the stressful periods, keeping your immune system strong.

Smile and Laugh! The old saying may actually be true: "Smile and the world smiles with you." Sometimes we have to force ourselves to smile or laugh in order to get started. Call an old friend, put in a funny movie, let out a laugh—as fake as it may be at first, it is likely to turn into true laughter.

Getting Started

We all have stress, and we handle it in different ways. I believe that attempting to follow the Ten Commandments of Ultimate Health actually reduces my stress. I am busier than ever before, and daily life is stressful — messy house, overbooked schedule, meeting my kids' needs, and various deadlines. During these times, I take comfort in these health commandments. They provide a structure that assures me that there are good things happening. Starting our day by taking supplements and eating a healthy breakfast gives me the sense that we are off to a good start each day. Praying, going to sleep earlier, drinking lots of water . . . all good things that provide calm during stressful periods.

For the practicals, go back to Dr. Pitman's five points above!

TENTH COMMANDMENT:
OPEN YOURSELF TO EMOTIONAL AND SPIRITUAL HEALING

"Lord my God, I called to you for help, and you healed me."
(Psalm 30:2)

"The Lord sustains them on their sickbed and restores them from their bed of illness." (Psalm 41:3)

"Lord, by such things people live; and my spirit finds life in them too. You restored me to health and let me live." (Isaiah 38:16)

The last health commandment is a big one, and an important one when it comes to healing. It is emotional and spiritual healing. Emotional healing occurs when we face the challenges, traumas, losses, and pain in our life. When we no longer allow ourselves to live in denial, within the layers of pain, we can begin to heal emotionally. Spiritual healing happens only through God.

Emotional pain is tough! It is tough to deal with but even harder to carry around. Think of Linus, the Peanuts character created by Charles Schulz. Linus is smart and well-liked, but he carries his blanket with him everywhere — wherever he goes. If you've been around a child who is very attached to his or her blanket, you know these tattered pieces of once-new fabric often smell, have holes, and are just downright gross. Everyone wants Linus to be free from the blanket. His sister, Lucy, even tried to bury it in the backyard. Linus himself probably wants to be free from it, but he just can't let it go.

I find that many patients are like Linus. Just as Linus hangs onto his blanket (probably without even realizing it), so many of us hang onto our pain. Our human nature holds onto the negative things in life. We could have truckloads of good things happen, but when one bad thing occurs, all the good things are all erased.

Physiologically, the part of the brain called the hippocampus is responsible for this. It holds on to the memories of life like a picture, even once the experience is over. When something negative happens, our brain's survival mechanism kicks in. The hippocampus prioritizes the negative memory as more important than all of the positive memories because it wants us to remember the trauma so that we can avoid it in the future. This survival mechanism is the reason one negative picture can dominate all of the positive pictures.[48]

These negative pictures held by the brain can lead us into cycles of fear, guilt, and shame. These feelings can limit us from creating new positive experiences. Spiritually, the enemy loves to keep us in fear, guilt, and shame. All of the positive things in life can be blocked by these negative feelings. Even physical healing can be blocked by fear, guilt, and shame.

How do we break this cycle? How do we become spiritually and emotionally whole again? The strategies for receiving emotional and spiritual healing are easier said than done, but they are all important to achieving ultimate health.

Face the Challenge: Sometimes we are very aware of the source of our pain. It might come from divorce, a death, a job loss, or other disappointment. Other times, we are not even consciously aware of the source of the pain. We have pushed it so far down or rationalized it, but it still manifests itself through actions, addictions, or physical illness. When I have patients that have tried to bury their pain so deep that they are not aware of the source of it, I suggest prayer and journaling. By asking God to reveal the source of the pain, it is more likely you can deal with it directly.

Once we face the challenges, we sometimes discover that these challenges are meant to change and redirect us. Everyone has pain and suffering, but sometimes pain is a way to move us toward or away from something. My friend, Ford Taylor, who wrote the testimonial at the beginning of this book, always says, "How much pain do you need to make a change?"

Learn to Forgive — Yourself and Others: The key to breaking the negative cycle of fear, guilt, and shame is forgiveness. If we are truly sorry, we are called to confess our sins and be confident in the Lord's forgiveness. We can then forgive ourselves, others, and the world. Forgiveness is easier said than done, but we are called to it. It is not an immediate process, and it helps to pray about it. As we heal our layers of stress, and we forgive, we will be released from fear, guilt, and shame and be able to live a happier, fuller life.

> Forgiveness is easier said than done, but we are called to it. It is not an immediate process, and it helps to pray about it.

Look for the Blessings in Disguise: I think of Laura Story's song Blessings.[49] Go to many online lyric sites and review the words to this song; they are quite moving and say so much about dealing with disappointment. If we allow them, our major disappointments can lead to better things. A young person is devastated by a broken heart but ends up meeting someone else much better suited for them. A person loses a job but finds a new one that leads them closer to God's purposes for their life. A car wreck brings a struggling family closer together. An individual struggles with an illness but learns to rely on God through the process. A young boy is so angry over the death of his grandfather that he develops a healing protocol to help thousands of others.

I could give 1,000 more examples. Blessings in disguise happen daily. Thank God for your trials, and ask Him to help you see these disguised blessings.

Work for Positive Reframing: Considering our brain holds on to the negative pictures in our lives as a protective mechanism, we have to work toward positive reframing. Just as you typically frame happy photographs, we have to frame the positive mental pictures of our lives. Remember the good things that have happened in your life. Adopt an attitude of gratitude for everything in your life and practice focusing on the positive. The power of attitude and thought drives our systems daily; our daily thoughts influence our lives toward the positive or the negative. By focusing on the positive, we will no longer be stuck by the negativity that our brain holds on to, and we can begin to anticipate God's blessings.

Build Relationships: Our mission daily is to keep the good things going. To do this, we need to welcome others in our journey and allow positive relationships in our lives. We all need to hold a hand until we can walk on our own. Once we are strong enough to walk on our own, we should hold someone else's hand. We should build relationships that please God. By building close and accepting relationships, we are building a safety net that will support us during our healing process. Seek out a minister. Join a prayer group. Build relationships in His name!

Surrender: God can heal us right now, instantly! Why doesn't this instant healing happen all the time? I believe that this type of healing only happens when we totally — and I do mean *totally* — surrender everything. Once we let go of every ounce of strength, we can be fixed.

Let go! Learn from Linus! Remember that the things we hold on to (our control, our power, our free will) . . . are tattered and worthless. Sometimes it's the things that we hold on to that actually block us from healing. We are so busy trying to fix things ourselves, we need to step back and let God lead us. The old adage of "Let go and let God" is a great reminder of the practice of surrender!

Scripture says: "After you have suffered a little while, [he] will himself restore you and make you strong, firm and steadfast. To him be the power forever and ever. Amen" (1 Peter 5:10, 11). Notice that

Peter doesn't say *some* of the power. Surrender is a great act of faith. It is realizing that we are broken and have no true control, and that can be scary. It is admitting that God knows what is best for us even if, in the moment, we disagree. Remember that God's kingdom is vast and mysterious. We don't know or understand all that He knows, so we need to rely on Him. The great news is that God loves us and that will never change.

Tools to help you surrender and listen to the Holy Spirit include praying, reading the Scriptures, and journaling.

Patiently Peel and Heal: Patients often come to my office for a physical illness. When that particular sickness is resolved, sometimes another illness "springs up." It seems like a case of bad luck, but this is actually a sign that whole-body healing is occurring. In simplified terms, the body realizes that one issue has been resolved, so it starts sending signals (or symptoms) that there is another issue that needs attention. This sometimes happens when dealing with emotional trauma. As one thing is resolved, another painful memory may surface.

When healing begins to occur, it is like peeling an onion. If you cut an onion in half, you see many layers surrounding the inside. Like an onion, we have layers that must be peeled away — emotional pain, sin, loss, illness . . . until the middle of the onion is reached. The middle of an onion is rose-shaped, a reminder of all the beautiful things that God has to offer. It represents God's healing.

It is important to remember that whole-person healing isn't just about resolving one physical or emotional issue; it is peeling away at layers. This can take time, but with every layer we are getting closer to ultimate health. Many times, this discourages patients at the beginning of their healing process. Yet as they continue to peel and heal, they realize that even though the process is not always quick, there is great value in the journey. As every layer is lifted — emotional pain, physical illness, and spiritual separation — they learn, grow, and begin to live the life God intended.

Follow the Ten Commandments of Ultimate Health: The Ten

Commandments of Ultimate Health can enable you to tread water during a crisis, helping you to maintain physical and emotional health. Perhaps the crisis is over and you are still not feeling grounded yet. The health commandments provided in this book can lead you back to a peaceful and healthy place. I am including some Scriptures that a great and godly friend gave to me. I find that reviewing these daily inspires the discipline needed to live the Ten Commandments of Ultimate Health. And they are, in general, Scriptures to live by as well:

> Perhaps the crisis is over and you are still not feeling grounded yet. The health commandments provided in this book can lead you back to a peaceful and healthy place.

Romans 8:28 – "And we know that in all things God works for the good of those who love him, who have been called according to his purpose."

Romans 8:16-18 – "…we share in his sufferings in order that we may also share in his glory."

1 Thessalonians 5:16-18 – "Rejoice always, pray continually, give thanks in all circumstances; for this is God's will for you in Christ Jesus."

Philippians 4:4 – "Rejoice in the Lord always. I will say it again. Rejoice!."

2 Corinthians 12:8-10 – "For when I am weak, then I am strong."

James 1:2 – "Consider it pure joy . . . whenever you face trials of many kinds."

* * * * *

God will bless you if you follow the Ten Commandments of Ultimate Health. Finally, we must open ourselves and remember that all things are possible with God.

Through the healing power of Jesus Christ, I have seen many miracles take place in my office, and I believe that there are many more miracles waiting to happen.

LORI'S SPIRITUAL HEALING

Dr. Pitman led me closer to God by bringing me back to nature. I was a prisoner to my allergies and asthma. There were times when I couldn't take a breath. When you can't breathe, you are afraid. I never took a walk that I wasn't afraid. I asked God to give me a normal, healthy immune system. I prayed for it and I wrote it down, knowing that it was impossible. I put my prayer request in front of me every day. It was impossible because the medical world only treats symptoms, and I couldn't imagine getting truly better. I didn't know Dr. Pitman existed, but I soon learned about him from a relative. After six months of seeing Dr. Pitman, I no longer had asthma. I can breathe in God's beauty, outside or inside, every second of every day. There was an emotional healing, too, as I am no longer afraid. Now instead of fear, I trust.

—L. Bernard, Cincinnati

Getting Started

When getting started on your emotional and spiritual journey, I recommend relying on God and asking him to send you others to support you on your journey.

When my boys were sick, I was not quite myself. I had been sleep deprived for almost a year, was sick of seeing my children suffer, tired of cooking every morsel of their food from scratch, broke, and broken. I was half sane (at best). But I relied heavily on my relationships with others and with God. In the darkest of hours, I could feel the presence of God with me, stronger than ever before.

I also started praying for friendships that could support me on this journey, and miraculously, old and new friends started showing up at my door. I remember thinking my neighbor Jenny was on a direct line with

God. When things were at their worse, she showed up at my door, ready to clean my house, babysit, or offer moral support. There were many other family members and friends who were integral to my survival.

Once the health crisis was over, I still was not myself. It was time for the emotional and spiritual healing to begin. Emotionally, I was a wreck. I was terrified that another life-threatening allergy was going to show up. I was waiting for the next phase of illness.

Again, I relied heavily on my support group. Conversation after conversation, this support group listened and lifted me up during this time of emotional healing. "Try to trust," my sister would say. "I know it is hard, but He has led you this far." Little by little, I began to trust, and I became emotionally renewed.

Spiritually, I was so grateful to God for healing my children that I wanted to make Him more of a focal point in my life. I asked God for forgiveness for my transgressions, and I am trying to live better. I am far from perfect, but I want to keep alive the relationship with God that I found during my darkest moments!

I am so grateful to God. He heals, forgives, and renews.

PART THREE

THE TEN COMMANDMENTS OF ULTIMATE HEALTH AND MORBIFIC STIMULI

Now that you are empowered with the tools to lead a healthy life, you must also be aware of the unhealthy world around us. The Ten Commandments of Ultimate Health are action steps you can take to improve your health, and *morbific stimuli* are the things you should try to avoid.

Think of Moses. He must have felt empowered to have the biblical Ten Commandments in his hand. Imagine his excitement as he made his way down the mountain. After spending 40 days on the mountain, he forgot about the ways of world down below. He was not prepared for what he saw when he finally made his way to his people. When he made it down the mountain and saw the idolatry and sin going on in the Israelite camp (Exodus 32), he threw down the Ten Commandments, shattering them. Even Moses, a great man of faith, lost his composure when he came face-to-face with the challenges of the world.

This section on morbific stimuli is to prepare you for the world in which we live so that you won't lose your enthusiasm for the Ten Commandments of Ultimate Health. When the world around you becomes too much, pick up this book and remember that even Moses had to pick up his tablets and start again.

MORBIFIC STIMULI

A six-year-old boy was taunting his younger brother. Making a claw out of his hand, he said, "This is a deadly monster." His four-year-old brother laughed.

Surprised that the claw-shaped hand didn't scare him, the older brother said in a low voice, "Do you know what *deadly* means?" Without waiting for an answer he moved the claw toward his brother and said, "It means it can kill you."

The youngest boy started to cry and ran out of the room screaming, "I didn't want to know what deadly was. . . . I didn't want to know!"

Sometimes, as adults, we don't want to know the information about what can harm us, either. Like my young patient, the four-year-old, we can laugh off or ignore something that we don't truly understand. Once we know more information about something, we can become uncomfortable and afraid.

The same is true of morbific stimuli. Morbific stimuli are things that can cause disease and death. They are all around us. Discussing morbific stimuli sometimes makes my patients want to go screaming out of the room. Once we gain information about them, we are forced to make uncomfortable decisions; however, learning about it can save our lives. Unlike the hand of the six-year-old boy, morbific stimuli can kill us whether we know about them or not—so we might as well become educated.

When I'm speaking in front of a group of people, I notice that there are always audience members who begin rolling their eyes when we discuss morbific stimuli. I have wondered if they feel that they cannot avoid everything that is bad for us — or maybe they feel that they have heard it all before.

> Sometimes, as adults, we don't want to know the information about what can harm us either. Like my young patient, the four-year-old, we can laugh off or ignore something that we don't truly understand.

My list of morbific stimuli includes allergies, viruses, bacteria, parasites, fungus and yeast, chemicals, radiation, emotional stress, dental injuries, and heavy metals. I agree that we cannot avoid everything that is unhealthy, but I know we can eliminate a whole lot of it.

It is not possible to avoid everything that is unhealthy for us, but step by step, little by little, we can clean up our households and our bodies. This book is meant to be a tool to take these incremental steps toward a healthier life.

In this final section, we'll step through each of ten things on my list of morbific stimuli—how they can hurt you, and what you can do about them.

ALLERGIES

Often, when someone sneezes or coughs, you hear them say, "Oh . . . it's just allergies." I always wonder: do they realize that allergies can be a big deal? I have had many patients who are completely immobilized because of their allergies. Their life has come to a virtual halt; they are severely restricted because of the severity of their allergies.

Allergies are immune system reactions that occur because the body comes in contact with an otherwise harmless substance; however, the immune response itself can be harmful to the body.

My practice treats the root cause of an allergy through:
• NAET (Nambudripad's Allergy Elimination Technique)
• EDS (Electro Dermal Screening), also known as biofeedback
• chiropractic adjustments
• emotional release techniques
• nutritional supplements
• purification

Many people are suffering from an allergy that is not detected by a typical allergy test. Various diseases, from chronic fatigue to autism, may simply be the way a body is reacting to the things it is coming in contact with in the environment. This chart shows the many different ways that allergies can manifest.

Allergies Can Manifest As . . .

Addiction	Fatigue
Anxiety	Hives
Appetite issues	Hyperactivity
Asthma	Hypoglycemia
Attention deficit disorder	Insomnia
Autism	Itching
Chronic fatigue	Leaky gut syndrome
Colitis	Learning issues
Cravings	Memory issues
Depression	Migraines
Diarrhea	Mood issues
Digestion issues	Night sweats
Dyslexia	Parasites
Ear infections	Phobias
Eczema	Sinusitis

It is commonly believed that allergies are limited to pollen, mold, weeds, pets, or foods. While these are common allergies, a body can develop an allergy to almost anything, including antibiotics, chemicals, computers, drugs, food, heat/cold, pets, plastics, radiation, and even another person.

Throughout my 28 years in practice, it is becoming apparent that allergies develop in many ways. A few of these are: overmedication, emotional trauma, genetic weaknesses, and possibly vaccines.

Overmedication Can Cause Allergies

When you take a drug, it alters your body. In fact, that is the reason you take the medication. But along with altering a specific and intended site and function, the drug is making its way through the entire body, potentially impacting multiple body systems in unintended ways. When you read a drug label that lists potential side effects, you're reading about reported unintended effects of the medication.

One of the unintended consequences a drug or medication can cause is that it can confuse your digestive system. Many of the medicines we use today come from herbs or plants. In their natural state these medicinal properties are surrounded with additional nutrients and natural buffers, such as minerals and liver enzymes for the body. When we extract medicine without using the whole plant, our body gets a super dose of the medicine without the natural buffers. In the digestive system, the medicine causes an imbalance between the yeast and bacteria that live in the gut. The natural symbiotic relationship in the colon terrain is disrupted. Without this balance, your immune system begins to attack, and sometimes it attacks things that are not harmful, causing an allergy.

> Without this balance, your immune system begins to attack, and sometimes it attacks things that are not harmful, causing an allergy.

Emotional Trauma Can Cause Allergies

To understand allergies and the root of the medical problem, it is necessary to understand how allergies develop. Our bodies are made up of cells. Each cell has memory, including the memory of emotional experiences. The cells of the immune system have been inadvertently conditioned to respond to otherwise harmless stimuli as if they were enemy invaders, manifesting in physical symptoms such as allergies.

For example, a woman came to my office with an undetected allergy, and I discovered she was allergic to her diamond engagement ring. Subsequently, she reported that many of her symptoms started when she broke off a wedding engagement in her early 20s. Even though she was now happily married, her body remembered the trauma of a broken engagement and had become allergic to diamonds. We treated her for an allergy to diamonds, and she was able to wear her new ring without symptoms.

If the root of the allergy is not dealt with, the underlying trauma will cause more allergies to develop. A woman came into my practice because she was allergic to her clothes. Her complexion was gray and she was no longer able to hold a job or have a social life. Slowly, through NAET treatments, her healthy color came back, and I discovered that the root of this patient's problems was a history of abuse as a child. Her body was holding on to those memories of abuse. She became allergic to things that reminded her of the time that she was abused. Eventually, her body couldn't stop reacting, and she developed even more allergies. After facing her trauma, going through NAET treatments, and implementing the Ten Commandments of Ultimate Health, she is free of her debilitating allergies.

Genetic Weaknesses

Often we are aware of the allergies that are handed down from one generation to the next. I frequently hear patients say, "I have my Dad's allergies" or "I have allergies . . . so does everyone in my family."

There is no doubt that we are predisposed to allergies through genetics. Recently a gene, named FCER1A, has been identified as the gene that encodes IgE (immunoglobulin E) receptors. In other words, this encoding gene indicates what the IgE response to a particular substance is going to be for that individual—and potentially for his or her future generations.

The good news is that even allergies that are passed down can be treated and alleviated with NAET. In my practice, I have treated not just families, but entire relationships, relieving them from living with debilitating allergies. Recently, the success I had healing one child from severe allergies brought in not only his aunts and uncles, but his great aunts and uncles and second cousins as well! This family had suffered for generations from a genetic weakness that I believe will be halted by NAET.

Vaccines

Can vaccines cause allergies? To understand how a vaccine might cause an allergy, it is important to understand *haptens*. A hapten is a substance that is, by itself, harmless — such as dust or dander — but when paired with another antigenic substance, such as a virus or bacteria, can elicit an immune response.

Haptens are used to create vaccines. There are some bacteria that are not recognized by the immune system of an infant; therefore, the bacteria of a typically harmless substance such as soy is disguised in a hapten.

In the case of the Prevnar shot, the seven strains of bacterium (Streptococcus Pneumonia) are kept alive in a soy culture.[50] Diptheria bacteria are grown in a yeast culture.[51] Is it possible that some infants create antibodies not only to the bacteria, but to soy as well?

In 2009, a group of scientists solved a research problem: scientists previously had been unable to study peanut allergies in mice.[52] Prior to this study, mice did not have allergic reactions to peanuts. The researchers paired peanut with a bacteria multiple times and the mice created antigens to the peanut—and thus developed peanut allergies. But not only did this cause the mice to be ready for use in a peanut-allergy study, it demonstrated the harmful impact of pairing food with bacteria or viruses multiple times as occurs in the case of vaccines given in a series of three shots or more.

Vaccination is a tough subject for people to talk about. Nonetheless, I will state that I believe there needs to be a constant push for safer vaccines. Unfortunately, the vaccination process is one-size-fits-all, and not every child is the same. Our culture has gotten to the point that it is taboo to question a vaccine or a vaccination schedule. Many states force their school children to be vaccinated, and most hospitals terminate workers who do not get the flu shot.

I have had patients who are injured by vaccines because they develop severe allergies or their bodies can't process the vaccine in its intended way. I believe we need to find ways to protect the weak — those who can't handle vaccinations — and the subject should never be too taboo to be discussed.

> I believe we need to find ways to protect the weak, those who can't handle vaccinations—and the subject should never be too taboo to be discussed.

Success with NAET

So let's talk about NAET (Nambudripad's Allergy Elimination Technique, as previously mentioned) and how every allergy, I believe, can be eliminated with this treatment. We have had great success using NAET to treat allergies in my practice. NAET is a drug-free treatment technique, and there are no shots involved. It utilizes acupuncture points to reintroduce a substance to the body. The patient avoids the substance for 25 hours and in most cases is able to tolerate the substance after the NAET treatment.

Sometimes an individual will need more than one treatment, but NAET eventually works for all substances. This is a permanent allergy elimination technique that will lead to a greater quality of life for those suffering from any kind of allergy.

CINDY'S TESTIMONIAL

Allergies and sinus infections have been a way of life for me. I started getting allergy shots at the age of seven. Puberty was not kind to me; my hormones went crazy. I had migraines, PMS, anxieties, and more.

About the time I turned 40, my allergies kicked in to super high gear. My sinuses felt swollen day and night. I experienced migraines that kept getting stronger and more frequent. My babies were one and three years old at the time.

The first food allergy I identified was a reaction to refined sugar. Soon I couldn't eat ice cream without getting a migraine. My allergies snowballed. The next item crossed off my "to eat" list was red meat, followed by tomatoes and then citrus. Soon eating anything processed would give me a terrible migraine.

I tried allergists, ENTs (ear, nose, and throat doctors), and acupuncturists. I was packing my food and taking it with me everywhere we went. Vacations were challenging and eating out was a chore. I was slowly being isolated from society because of my awful migraines and food sensitivities.

For 12 years I continued to eliminate foods; I experienced three to five migraines a week. My friendships were suffering, and I was so depressed. I felt like I was living a life sentence. Every day was a struggle.

Six months ago my food choices were limited to pork, chicken, vegetables, and some fruits. Even on that strict diet, my migraines kept coming three to five times a week. One day I was out to lunch with a friend — my lunch was packed, of course — and she told me about two boys who suffered like I did — and also packed their lunches. Except now they were eating more foods again, she said.

I was on the phone immediately, talking to their mom to find out how they were able to get rid of their food allergies. I was told about Dr. Pitman and his allergy treatments. I have been going to him for only seven months, but my healing is amazing.

I have utilized most of the services offered in the office, including the cranial sacral work, chiropractic care, nutritional testing, and NAET. I have received 25 NAET treatments so far; I've been allergic to everything Dr. Pitman has tested me for.

*Slowly, I am **adding foods** back into my diet. Before Dr. Pitman, I* *could not even touch an orange. Now I can eat one! My citrus allergy was very strong. Instead of the typical 25-hour abstinence after the NAET treatment, I had to wait 50 hours to clear citrus.*

My migraines are going away too! I now have one to two migraines a month as opposed to three to five a week! Dr. Pitman took many of the modalities I was familiar with (acupressure, chiropractic care, supplementation) and put them together to provide healing to my body.

I was cautiously optimistic that my allergies could be treated. I was surprised with all the additional healing I received:

- *The cranial work relieved my anxiety. I was always uptight and nervous.*
- *I have been weaned off of four medications: Bystolic (a heart medicine), Nasonex (for allergies), Sudafed (for allergies), and an osteoporosis medicine.*
- *I have reduced my Estroven dose by half.*
- *I have really been working my dose of Effexor XR down over time. I was on a 150 mg dose for anxiety and depression. I am down to a 27.5 mg dose.*
- *I have always had chicken skin—now that is gone.*

I came to Dr. Pitman to get relief from my food allergies and migraines. What I got was my life back!

— ***Cindy Flesch, Kentucky***

AN EXAMPLE OF NAET TREATING AUTISM

Kelly was a pharmacist, but after her son Logan was born, she had to quit her job. She couldn't figure out why her son would not sleep. The most Logan would sleep was 15 minutes at a time, and the rest of the time he mostly cried.

As time went on, Logan was not meeting his milestones. Finally, at 18 months, Kelly saw a TV show about autism and realized that was what Logan was living with: autism. Logan had speech and occupational therapy three to five times a week. When he turned five they started a gluten- free/casein-free diet, which showed huge improvements. Eventually Logan was weaned off the gluten-free/casein-free diet and only certain trigger foods were avoided.

Kelly used her research skills and prayer to search out new therapies and treatments. She always knew there was a connection between Logan's allergies and his autism. As she studied, Kelly became very interested in NAET treatments. She was the pharmacist who was determined to never medicate Logan unless she absolutely had too. After searching the Internet when Logan was 11 years old, Kelly found my practice.

My office was two hours away, but she was determined to give the NAET treatments a try. By Logan's third treatment he had a calmness about him that has remained to this day. He was able to eat a piece of bread without getting giggly. He no longer wanted to raid the kitchen cabinets. The unhealthy weight fell off as his body was healed.

Cranial sacral and nutritional treatments were also done through my office. After each treatment Logan continues to show even more improvement.

Logan has had 43 NAET treatments over the past three years. Kelly has noticed that he:

- can sit longer and is calmer.
- has gone from having a full-time assistant at school to merely having someone in the room to keep him on task.
- has improved his language to the point that he and his mother can carry on conversations!
- is now normal weight for his height; when he started NAET he was very overweight.
- has no allergy issues; in the past his allergies were so bad he could not breathe.
- is rarely sick; before the treatments Logan was often sick.
- has no intestinal issues; Logan had horrible issues such as passing gas and horrible-smelling bowel movements.

• has eliminated most or all of his bad eating habits. Before his treatments Logan craved carbohydrates constantly. He was always in the pantry and the refrigerator. That too has stopped.

Kelly's pharmaceutical background led her to initially believe that only conventional doctors and medicine could help her son. What she has found is that care like the NAET treatments I gave her son can, and has, tremendously increased Logan's quality of life. The NAET treatments have expanded Logan's world and his ability to assimilate himself into that world.

VIRUSES

Two people receive an email alerting them there are thousands of computer viruses spreading wildly throughout the country. One person checks her antivirus software and makes sure it is in place and working. Next, she checks her computer firewalls and increases overall security. The other person doesn't have antivirus software or a firewall setup on his computer. He tries to download the necessary software and finds out it is too late . . . his computer is already infected.

When it comes to your computer, which person are you? Have you done your best to prevent a virus? When it comes to your body, which person are you? I find that most of my new patients do more to prevent viruses on their computers than they do to prevent them in their bodies.

Viruses are submicroscopic agents that are unable to grow or reproduce outside a host cell. Viruses do not have a cell wall of their own, so they find the weakest area in your cell to make a cell wall for themselves. Then the viruses go into your tissues to replicate themselves. They can go into cells in your brain, heart, nervous system — anywhere in your body.

Examples of viral infections are chicken pox, measles, rotavirus, H1N1, and the common cold.

The best defense against viruses is a good offense. If you prepare your immune system properly, it should be able to defend itself well against viruses. You can't depend on vaccinations to protect your body. There are millions of viruses, most of which do not have vaccinations. Strengthening and preparing your immune system daily, similar to preparing your computer for an attack, is the best way to handle the pesky viruses that surround us all the time.

> Antibiotics cannot kill viruses; therefore, when you take an antibiotic when you have a virus, you compromise your immune system even more.

Antibiotics do not work on viruses. Antibiotics work by breaking down the cell wall around a bacterial cell. Since viruses do not have a cell wall, antibiotics have nothing to attack. Antibiotics cannot kill viruses; therefore, when you take an antibiotic when you have a virus, you compromise your immune system even more. Now your body still has to fight the virus, but is also left dealing with the antibiotic floating around in your intestine. The antibiotic ends up killing the good bacteria in your gut that is needed in the battle against the virus. This can become a vicious cycle.

Today's children are routinely prescribed antibiotics for viral ear infections. This practice starts early in a child's life and can lead to many problems down the road. Here is how this typically plays out in the lives of American children: The first sign of a viral ear infection is that the ear canal gets red. Parents rush to the doctor to get an antibiotic to help their child's ear pain go away. The antibiotic does not kill the virus, but it does kill the good bacteria in the gut. When the good bacteria in the gut are depleted, yeast grows and causes fungal infections. The next week the mother and patient are back because the child is still sick. Now the child still has the viral ear infection and a fungal infection from the antibiotic from the first week. Each additional antibiotic weakens the child's immune system, further spiraling into the vicious cycle.

Many childhood ailments are caused from this cycle. One child in my practice with a range of problems, including allergies, autistic symptoms, and hearing issues, had been on 22 antibiotics for ear infections in his first two years of life.

I have found that the cause of most childhood ear infections is a misalignment of the C1 and C2 main vertebrae in the neck. This misalignment blocks the lymphatic drainage system. This blockage allows fluid to build up in the ear canal instead of draining naturally. This fluid becomes infected because it is static and the body cannot get rid of it. Babies should have a light chiropractic adjustment soon after birth to align the atlas and the axis, preventing this cycle of ear infections.

Once you get a virus, there are homeopathic remedies that can treat the virus and even the flu within 24 to 36 hours. The immune system is weakened from the virus, and the terrain of the body is congested, allowing the virus to live within our bodies. Change the terrain with supplementation, and you can change the virus.

The best prevention of viruses is following the Ten Commandments of Ultimate Health. There are hundreds of immunizations, but there are millions of viruses. Immunizations can't provide protection against them all, so strengthening your immune system is your best defense. Following the Ten Commandments of Ultimate Health, combined with basic hygiene, provides your best shot at avoiding and beating viruses.

* * * * *

A NURSE'S TESTIMONY

As a nurse and a mother of three kids, I have found alternative medicine helpful. Conventional medicine has little to offer when your kids are beginning to get sick, but supplements can boost our immune systems and often reduce the duration of the illness. When my 12-year-old, a patient of Dr. Pitman's, starts to feel a cold or cough come on, he takes the initiative to take myrrh. Considering myrrh is not the best-tasting thing, it is amazing that he requests it. He does it because he knows it helps, and he is more likely to get better quicker.

— ***M. Gieseke, RN***

BACTERIA

B acteria are prolific! There are approximately 10 times as many bacterial cells as there are human cells in the body. Fortunately, the majority of bacterial cells are rendered harmless by the protective effects of the human immune system.

Pathogenic bacteria includes bacterial meningitis, cholera, strep, MRSA, and leprosy. The signs of a bacterial infection are fever, swelling, soreness, and possibly vomiting and diarrhea. E. coli and salmonella are food-borne bacterial infections that can also be dangerous.

Bacteria do have a cell wall, so antibiotics can be used effectively when there is an outbreak of these bacterial infections. When necessary, antibiotics are life saving. Natural medicine also has ways to fight mild bacterial infections such as mild silver protein, myrrh, sambucas, and berberine; however, these should be dosed specifically by a trained natural medicine practitioner, and done so according to age, weight, and the specific infection. Antibiotics are the big guns in our war with bacteria and need to be used only when necessary.

We are jeopardizing our future. The overuse of antibiotics is creating super bugs that are antibiotic-resistant. Our yeast-filled bodies have compromised immune systems. We need not use antibiotics lightly. Through my practice, I have become acquainted with a family who lost their mother to MRSA (methicillin-resistant Staphylococcus aureus) after childbirth. The maternity ward had a MRSA outbreak; three mothers caught the infection, and one died from it. After speaking with the family, I learned that the mother who died was under a great deal of stress and had many attacks to her immune system while she was pregnant. Her depleted body couldn't defend against the super bug, even with the help of antibiotics.

> We are jeopardizing our future. The overuse of antibiotics is creating super bugs that are disease-resistant.

Bacteria in Our Food: Throughout the last 20 years, there have been numerous nationwide recalls of food containing harmful bacteria. E. coli is no longer just in beef; it is being discovered in apple juice, spinach, and other random produce items distributed throughout the country. The E. coli in the produce items is due to the waste products that run off from the factories into the fields, contaminating even our freshest foods.

The risk of getting E. coli from beef is also increasing. The way foods are processed today, there may be the DNA of thousands of cows within one American hamburger, so the risk for E. coli increases exponentially. Documentaries such as *Food, Inc.* have brought to light the horrible conditions in our country's food processing plants.[53]

Kevin's Law is proposed legislation that would give the U.S. Department of Agriculture the power to close down plants that produce contaminated meat. Kevin's Law was named in memory of two-year-old Kevin Kowalcyk, who died in 2001 after eating a hamburger contaminated with E. coli. This law would give the USDA the authority to enforce its own standards by shutting down plants that continually breach basic health standards. Today, Kevin's

Law has not been passed and our food still has a great chance of being contaminated.

The more you know about where your food comes from, the better off you will be. Visit not only your farmer but the processor of the meat you are purchasing. The best way to protect yourself and your family is to truly know where your food was grown and where it has been.

The best protection against bacteria is to strengthen the bacterial balance in the colon by following the Ten Commandments of Ultimate Health.

PARASITES

In Cincinnati, Ohio, where I live and practice, parasites are a concern when going to bed. In Ohio, bedbugs are becoming an epidemic. Bedbugs are pesky parasites that feed on blood and borough into our beds until the next night, when they suck our blood again. People are disturbed by the images of bedbugs that are occasionally shown on the evening news. As disgusting as parasites are in your bed, they are equally troubling in your body.

No matter where you live, you are not immune to parasites. Many people are concerned about parasites only when traveling overseas; however, there are many domestic parasites as well. If you swim, have pets, or eat undercooked food, it is very possible that you can get a parasite.

They can cause lower back pain, allergies, sinus problems, chronic fatigue, irritable bowel syndrome, and other gastrointestinal issues. They also can overwhelm your immune system and make you more susceptible to yeast overgrowth, bacteria, and viruses. Parasites can also deplete their host — you — from nutrition and hydration.

Some common parasites are trichinosis, tapeworm, and pinworm.

One of the best ways to prevent parasites is to know where your food comes from. Prepare your food in a safe manner. Wash your food well. Keep meat preparation separate from other foods you are preparing and cook your food well.

Parasites, in my opinion, are generally overlooked by the medical community in the United States. Blood tests and stool work are often not accurate for specific diagnose of parasites. It is best to test for parasites during the full moon as these pesky creatures, like other worms, become more active and reproduce at this time. A solid homeopathic practitioner can get rid of parasites with an herbal and homeopathic treatment in 40 days.

For hundreds of years, dandelions in the spring and black walnuts in the fall were gathered and used as antiparasitic homeopathic medicines. I don't recommend pulling dandelions today (as they are probably covered with weed-killer anyway), but I use nature's seasonal gifts as a reminder that parasites do exist and that occasional cleansing is needed to make certain our bodies are free from them.

* * * * *

PARASITES FROM A POOL

We thought my husband had caught a bad stomach bug when he was vomiting and had diarrhea for more than a week. I was starting to feel sick as well when I saw on the news that the pool at our local recreation center had the parasite cryptosporidium. I realized we had both been swimming there one day prior to the onset of our symptoms. Dr. Pitman advised me on what supplements to take to fight the parasite, and my vomiting and diarrhea stopped that day. It took me another day or two to completely have a strong stomach again, but after following Dr. Pitman's advice, the duration of my symptoms were significantly less than my husband's.

– L. B., Cincinnati, Ohio

FUNGUS / YEAST

Leviticus 14:37-39 talks about fungus: "[The priest] is to examine the mold on the walls, and if it has greenish or reddish depressions that appear to be deeper than the surface of the wall, the priest shall go out the doorway of the house and close it up for seven days. On the seventh day the priest shall return to inspect the house. If the mold has spread on the walls . . . "

Many translations describe this greenish and reddish substance as a fungus or a type of it — mildew and mold. The passage demonstrates that fungus has always been a nuisance.

Most fungi are visible to the naked eye. There are half a million different types of fungi! A common fungus is athlete's foot, caused by a ringworm infection. However, yeast is probably the most prolific fungus in our bodies.

Yeast is a beast, and it has been widely studied in the last 20 years. There are 1,500 different kinds of yeast. It is common problem in our country because yeast is living organisms that feed on alcohol and sugar. The typical American diet is full of alcohol and sugar. Once you have yeast, a diet of alcohol and sugar makes it so much worse.

Antibiotics also add to the yeast problem. Every time an antibiotic is used, the antibiotic kills off both the good and bad bacteria in the digestive system. Your body needs good bacteria to combat yeast. When this beneficial bacteria is killed off by the antibiotic, the yeast starts to multiply. After an antibiotic is used, the only way to replenish the fallen flora is through quality probiotic supplementation. If the flora is not quickly repopulated, yeast will take over the digestive system and cause many of the typical American maladies such as allergies, depression, fatigue, poor memory, mood swing, muscle aches, loss of libido, PMS, and weight gain.

> Yeast is a beast, and it has been widely studied in the last 20 years. There are 1,500 different kinds of yeast.

Our yeast-filled bodies have compromised immune systems. The over-prescription of antibiotics is causing our bodies to develop horrendous systemic yeast infections.

Yeast symptoms may be held at bay with prescriptions, but for true healing, yeast must be brought back into homeostasis in the body. Take a quality probiotic daily and improve your diet. Make sure the probiotic is fresh (not expired), and it should be refrigerated by your supplier as well as at home. Make sure it states that it is gluten-free and corn-free as gluten and corn actually inflame yeast. Don't take your probiotic with heated liquids, as the heat will kill the good bacteria in the probiotic.

To eliminate yeast, you need to starve it out of your body. When trying to eliminate yeast, I suggest a diet of that is abundant in vegetables, lean meat, low-glycemic fruits such as berries, and small quantities of brown rice.

Once you conquer the yeast beast that wreaks havoc for so many people, many adverse conditions and symptoms vanish.

* * * * *

LOUIS' STORY

When I came to Dr. Pitman's office, I had two issues. I had a platter-sized splotch on my abdomen that caused migratory itching throughout my body, and I also had IBS (irritable bowel syndrome). My IBS was becoming so severe that I had to plan my daily meals around business meetings in order to avoid getting sick in public. It was getting to the point that I had to plan hours ahead before leaving my house. I could not just pick up and leave.

A dermatologist tried to cover up my itch with a topical ointment, but it did little to improve my condition. Another MD was prescribing medications for my IBS. During a four-to-five-month period, I was taking quite a few medications with little relief.

After consulting with Dr. Pitman, an EDS (Electro Dermal Screening) test identified that I had yeast and fungus issues. I proceeded this testing with NAET treatments by taking supplements daily. At my 11th NAET treatment, I was treated for yeast and experienced significant results. It was the beginning of getting better.

Today I no longer have to deal with the itching throughout my body. The swelling on my abdomen has cleared up, and my IBS is significantly better. Ninety percent of my issues are resolved, and I have control of my life again!

— Louis, Cincinnati, Ohio

CHEMICALS

C hemicals are used around us all the time. There is no way to avoid chemical exposure. Our bodies need to be able to handle the environmental onslaught of these exposures every day. They are everywhere — in our water, food, places of work, and schools. Considering there are so many chemicals that we can't control, we must attempt to limit or avoid those we can.

Chemicals in Water: Our drinking water is contaminated with chemicals, hormones, and medications. In some counties in Ohio, you can actually taste the chlorine in the water. As discussed previously in the Ten Commandments of Ultimate Health, the best water is filtered through reverse osmosis. Don't allow your water to be contaminated with bacteria, viruses, pharmaceuticals, and parasites when a reverse osmosis system can be used as a simple, cost-effective solution.

Chemicals in Air: Just outside of Cincinnati, there is a plastics factory that released 500 pounds of chemicals due to a production accident; it was reported that about 157 pounds of the chemicals were cancer causing.[54] We do not have a great deal of control over the air we breathe, but we can consider it when choosing a home, and we can consider installing an air filtration system in our homes.

Chemicals in Foods: According to the Pesticide Action Network of North America, children exposed to pesticides face higher incidences of birth defects, childhood brain cancers, autism spectrum disorders (ASD), neurodevelopment delays, and endocrine system disruption. Pound for pound, children absorb a higher concentration of pesticides than adults. Researchers have found that an array of impaired brain and nervous system functions, including the ability to draw, were correlated to pesticide exposure during development.[55]

> Our sick children, suffering from autism, ADHD, and even cancer are telling us our environment is deadly.

Our children today are like the canaries in the old coal mines. Historically, coal miners sent the yellow canary into the coal mine to test the safety of the mine. If the level of gas was too high, the canary died and didn't come out, and the coal miners knew it was not safe for humans. Our sick children, suffering from autism, ADHD, and even cancer are telling us our environment is deadly.

Pesticides don't just affect children. A landmark 2010 report in environmental health news linked pesticides to the increased incidence of melanoma among adult farm workers.[56] Melanoma is a deadly skin cancer that has tripled in the United States in the last 30 years.[57] Some of the cancer-causing pesticides are approved for household use and may be in your home.

According to a 2011 Environmental Working Group article, the produce listed under the "Dirty Dozen" part of the chart below are the items with the most pesticides. Buy the organic version of these dirty dozen. The "Clean Fifteen" have the lowest amount of pesticides.[58]

The Dirty Dozen	The Clean Fifteen
Apples	Onion
Celery	Sweet corn
Strawberries	Pineapples
Peaches	Avocado
Spinach	Asparagus
Nectarines (imported)	Sweet peas
Grapes (imported)	Mangoes
Sweet bell peppers	Eggplant
Potatoes	Cantaloupe (domestic)
Blueberries (domestic)	Kiwi
Lettuce	Cabbage
Kale/collard greens	Watermelon
	Sweet potatoes
	Grapefruit
	Mushrooms

For more information about pesticides and your food, visit www. whatsonmyfood.org. This site will tell you all the pesticides found in each fruit and vegetable. To find out more about how each of the pesticides in these foods impacts your physical and mental health, visit www.pesticideinfo.org.

Food Chemicals: The Standard American Diet (SAD) is sad! Our food is laden with chemicals. As the richest nation in the world, we are also one of the sickest. Our ability to have such an abundant selection of foods has led to very poor eating habits.

First, we eat dead food. The processed foods we eat take energy out of our bodies to digest them. Living foods *give* our bodies energy as we eat them. The healthiest food at the grocery store is found around the perimeter of the store. Fresh fruits and vegetables, meats, dairy, and frozen produce are all from living things. The center aisles in the grocery store are full of processed boxed food, which is dead food.[59]

The flavorings seen on many labels (natural or artificial) are not flavorings but chemicals. Natural flavorings contain something natural from a plant or a spice, but can have many other chemicals combined with them. Even though natural flavorings are not good, artificial flavorings are worse. The most commonly known artificial flavoring is MSG (monosodium glutamate).

In September 2011, the reputable website www.mercola.com warned its followers to beware of natural flavor enhancers, as these are made from human embryonic kidney cells.[60] According to the Weston A. Price Foundation, some artificial flavorings are made with cloned, aborted fetal cells.[61] In preparation for this book, everyone who read a draft wondered if this could actually be true. I will tell you here what I told them: The bottom line is that if you are eating things with artificial flavors in them, you have no idea what you are ingesting. You are playing Russian roulette with your health.[62]

Even with all of the efforts of grassroots groups to have food properly labeled, companies can insist that their additives are proprietary and not include them on the label. For now, it is important to be cautious of items that have artificial flavorings. If you are buying packaged foods, it is best to buy organic.

> We know that artificial flavorings are bad for us. We also know that fresh, organic food gives our bodies energy and nutrition. So why do we continue to eat dead foods?

We know that artificial flavorings are bad for us. We also know that fresh, organic food gives our bodies energy and nutrition. So why do we continue to eat dead foods?

The advertising media directed at children and adults is an overwhelming purchasing stimulus. It creates false desires for the cheap, dead food that is advertised. For every dollar spent in advertising that tells us the benefits of eating fruits and vegetables, the food and beverage industry spends $1,100.[63]

Chemicals in Household Cleaners: Each home contains from three to eight gallons of hazardous materials in kitchens, bathrooms, garages, and basements. Examples include pesticides, herbicides, poisons, corrosives, solvents, fuels, paints, motor oil, antifreeze, mercury and mercury-containing wastes.[64] Other items like furniture polish, deodorants, and many cleaning products contain formaldehyde. Since 1979, the U.S. Consumer Product Safety Commission has demonstrated that formaldehyde causes cancer in lab animals.[65]

Marketplace, a Canadian investigative consumer show, measured volatile organic compounds in the typical household and found the average home has 50 parts per billion (ppb), noting that any cleaner measuring more than 500 ppb could be a problem for people with sensitivities. One popular household cleaner came in more than 1,000 times higher than the 500 ppb! Some disinfectants contain denatured ethanol that has been linked to nervous system depression and alkyl dimethyl benzyl ammonium chloride, a pesticide. One popular cleaner lists two pesticides, dimethyl benzyl ammonia chloride and dimethyl ethyl benzyl ammonia chloride.[66] This demonstrates that the amount of volatile compounds and pesticides are significant in common household cleaners.

Switch to safer cleaners. There are many ways to clean safely. Companies like Shaklee offer safe alternatives to the chemically laden grocery store cleaners. Other alternatives to chemical cleaners include baking soda, vinegar, lemon juice, and water. The Internet is a great place to find natural cleaning combinations for almost every situation. Doing some of this basic research will also remind you that there are many more people in the world looking for cleaning alternatives.

Chemicals on Your Skin: Your skin is the largest organ on your body. What you put on it . . . goes *in* it. Be cautious about the makeup, soap, and shampoo you are using. According to the

Environmental Working Group, public law allows almost any ingredient in personal care products and requires no safety testing of products or ingredients.[67] Check your labels carefully and investigate the products you are using. Many contain parabens and other toxic ingredients. Toluene is a cancer-causing chemical found in many nail care products and other cosmetics.[68] The list of toxic chemicals in health and beauty products is too long to list but can be found on www.cosmeticsdatabase.com. This site also allows you to look up the products you are currently using and find out if they are toxic for you.

> So while you are enjoying extra time in the sun, your body is being exposed to cancer rays.

One of the latest line of products to be concerned about is sunscreen. Sunscreens may contain harmful chemicals. In addition, sunscreen filters rays of the sun that cause sunburn, but not the cancer-causing rays of the sun. So while you are enjoying extra time in the sun, your body is being exposed to cancer rays. Without sunscreen, you would naturally stay out of the sun during the hottest hours—11 a.m. to 4 p.m.—to avoid being burned.

We also need to realize that our bodies need sunlight so that they can make their own, natural vitamin D. High vitamin D blood levels boost your immune system. Sunscreen inhibits our ability to make vitamin D. Currently, many studies are being validated that are linking sunscreen to cancer. If you are going to be out in the sun during those hottest hours of the day, use zinc oxide and make certain there are not additional chemicals in your sunscreen.

RADIATION

R adiation causes free radical damage to your cells, which makes you more prone for disease.

In order to understand how this happens, think back to your high school chemistry days. Atoms are the smallest part of all matter. Atoms are comprised of protons and neutrons in the nucleus surrounded by electrons that orbit the nucleus in rings. Atoms are considered "stable" if they have an even number of electrons in their outermost ring. For the element of oxygen, that would be six electrons in the second ring. Atoms can lose one of those electrons, causing the atom to be a "free radical" atom. It has lost an electron and now the atom is looking to "steal" an electron from another atom to gain stability again.

Radiation is one of the ways atoms lose electrons. Free radical atoms cause cell damage; as they lose electrons, they steal electrons from other atoms. All this losing and stealing weakens the cells and causes oxidative stress and eventually causes aging and illness.

Microwaves are a large source of radiation in the home. When you microwave foods, you are speeding up the cells in the food —

causing them to vibrate and create heat. This vibration causes the food to be hot, but it also changes the chemical makeup of the food. If you microwave in a plastic container, the atoms in the plastic speed up too. The chemicals come off your plastic and leach out into your food. Use ceramic or glass when using a microwave, and avoid the microwave whenever possible. Invest in a toaster oven.

> If you microwave in a plastic container, the atoms in the plastic speed up too. The chemicals come off your plastic and leach out into your food.

Any food that is hot can leach chemicals out of its container. Be careful to try not to use plates made in China — in any setting — and especially not in the microwave. Ceramics contain heavy metals, lead, and various other chemicals that are activated by the radiation.

Cell phones also emit radiation. You can put copper on the back of your phone to absorb some of the radiation. Be mindful of how much time you have a cell phone against your ear. The rate of brain tumors is increasing. Studies have shown that the cell signal is absorbed up to two inches into the adult skull. There is special concern about the risks in younger age groups, as cell phone signals penetrate much deeper into children's brains. In an article in *Journal of Assisted Tomography*, the authors suggest some steps that cell phone users can take to reduce exposure. These include limiting the number and length of calls, restricting children's cell phone use, communicating by text instead of voice, and wearing an "air tube" headset (not a regular wired headset) rather than holding the phone to the ear.[69]

You can also buy diodes to put on the phone to lower radiation, but copper is a cheap, easy fix.

Radiation sneaks into our lives in many forms. I had a patient who came to me after suffering for years from lesions all over her body. She wasn't able to find any relief from the conventional medical community. By testing her through electro dermal screening, I discovered that the lesions were caused from EFW's (electromagnetic frequency waves). After questioning her, I discovered that she slept with an electric blanket every night. She removed the blanket and the lesions disappeared.

Although we can't eliminate all forms of radiation, we can become educated about how they seep into our world and attempt to avoid them whenever possible.

EMOTIONAL STRESS

Have you ever heard the expression: "He or she died of heartbreak"? Did you ever know someone who died unexpectedly only a few short months after their spouse or child died? Emotional stress can kill you. For adults, long-term stress is the most dangerous. Eventually, your body is not able to function normally after these long periods. Long-term emotional stress is caused by the death of a spouse, death of a close family member, divorce, loss of your job, a major illness or injury, and post-traumatic stress.

Stress leads to exhaustion and nutritional depletion. It is important to support the physical body in order to let the emotional healing occur. Typically, supplementation includes supporting the endocrine system (adrenals, pituitary, and thyroid) as well as reducing the stress to the entire body through chiropractic care.

Many people bury their stress, but it manifests itself in areas such as addictions to food, alcohol, drugs, or sex. For others, stress can lead to unidentified physical illnesses. Sometimes the stress is buried so deeply that individuals do not understand what is causing their symptoms. Through biofeedback and electrodermal screening, the stress can be identified and addressed. It is also important to remember to surround yourself with people who will encourage, support, and pray for you.

> For adults, long-term stress is extremely dangerous. Eventually, your body is not able to function normally after these long periods.

Unlike the other morbific stimuli, these significant stressful events often cannot be avoided. The most important thing we can do is follow the Ten Commandments of Ultimate Health with diligence to protect ourselves during these times of extended stress. Refer back to the Ninth Commandment: Cope with Stress. The thoughts there will provide helpful reminders of how to deal with the challenges you are facing.

DENTAL INJURIES

Your teeth are vitally important to the health of your immune system. The study of reflexology uses the meridian pathways and acupuncture points in the foot to promote healing in all parts of the body. Similarly, your teeth are connected to every system in your body. Each tooth has a different corresponding organ, vertebra, joint, and part of the endocrine system.

Taking care of your teeth keeps your immune system intact.

Root Canals: Root canals remove more than just a rotted tooth. They also take away the nerve that is removed in the procedure. The nerve was used by the brain as an information pathway. Even after the nerve is gone, there can still be an infection that needs to be treated.[70]

The nerve in your tooth functions like the oil light in your car. It is an indicator and connector between the tooth and the brain. After a root canal, the removal of the nerve eliminates the oxygen, circulation, and immune system for that tooth.

Cancer researchers are discovering that there is a link between root canals and cancer.[71] Through electrodermal screening and biofeedback techniques, I have discovered that breast cancer can be caused from a root canal on the tooth that exists on the meridian of the breast. In fact, I have found that root canals are the cause of many symptoms that are misdiagnosed as something else. When the root canal is corrected with an intervention from a biological dentist, the symptoms are alleviated. Often the treatment is ozone therapy, which eliminates the bacteria in the infected area.

A good resource for more information on this is the book *Root Canal Cover-Up* by Dr. George Meinig.

Dental Fillings: For years there has been a debate of whether mercury fillings are harmful to the body. Even the FDA seems to vacillate on its stance of mercury amalgams, making a statement one year that it may have harmful effects and concluding the next year that it doesn't. The FDA's website is full of complaints from individuals who feel they have been harmed from mercury fillings. You can view these at www.FDA.org.

> Because of its toxicity, mercury has been phased out of almost every other consumer product: why do we still allow it to be inserted into our teeth?

Because of its toxicity, mercury has been phased out of almost every other consumer product: why do we still allow it to be inserted into our teeth?

Sadly, I had a patient who came into my office to find out why she had a miscarriage. The biofeedback results indicated that there had been mercury poisoning. My patient told me that she had been to the dentist the day before she miscarried and had a filling placed in her teeth.

Be aware that amalgams, known as silver tooth fillings, can be up to 50 percent mercury. You need to have a conversation with your dentist before every filling is placed in your mouth. If your dentist insists on using mercury, it is time to get up and leave. Better yet, ask the questions before your appointment. There are good composite options that are strong and affordable, and there is no reason to use silver amalgams with mercury in them any longer.

In my office, I use electrodermal screening to assess the level of stress on each of the body systems. Through this test I can determine if you have had harmful dental procedures done and how to correct them if so.

When there is a problem, I refer my patients to a biological dentist, a specialized dentist who can reduce the effects of mercury toxicity and root canal therapy. A biological dentist is often hard to find. If you discover a dental issue through EDS, the EDS practitioner may be able to refer you to trusted dentist. Other helpful websites include:

www.hugginsappliedhealing.com

www.holisticdental.org

www.iabdm.org.

I would also advise speaking to your current or new dentist. Question them about their philosophy before making your next appointment.

HEAVY METALS

In the 1930s, the negative effects of lead poisoning were witnessed. At the time, the United States allowed lead into its household paints, and children who ate the paint chips peeling from the wall were poisoned by them. This caused permanent mental retardation. It wasn't until the 1970s that lead was restricted in household paints.

Today, heavy metal poisoning can occur when a person comes in contact with a high amount of metals or is unable to metabolize the metals properly. Symptoms of heavy-metal poisoning can range from cognitive impairment to depression to other psychological disorders.

Common contact with heavy metals is often a result of the following: Mercury in dental compounds, metal cookware, processed food, deodorants and cosmetics, vaccines, and toxic air from environmental pollutants from factories.

Dental Compounds: Avoid mercury fillings and review the dental information in the previous chapter.

Cookware: Heavy metals can also be found in cookware. Stainless steel pans, cooking stones, and Pyrex and other glassware are your best bet for cooking. Also, avoid any cookware or plates that are made in China or India. Cookware made in these countries has much less stringent regulations than the U.S. on heavy metals that are allowed in paints. Unfortunately, many things in the typical kitchen today are not made in the U.S. — unless the cook puts a significant effort into researching the items before purchasing them.

Metals in Processed Foods: Food is processed on metal equipment that can leach into our foods, adding to our overall metal toxicity.

> Food is processed on metal equipment that can leach into our foods, adding to our overall metal toxicity.

Metals in Deodorants and Cosmetics: Aluminum is commonly used in deodorants and cosmetics. Check the safety of the products you are using at www.cosmeticsdatabase. com and avoid these toxic items. Switch to a natural deodorant or try using baking soda or a combination of baking soda and cornstarch for an effective and safe deodorant.

Toxic Air: Heavy metals from automobiles and factories can surround us, contaminating the air we breathe. It is important to cleanse our bodies through purification and supplementation to allow us to process these deadly toxins out of our bodies.

Vaccines: Vaccines have many more components in them than just a single virus or bacterium. Metals such as aluminum and thimerosal (mercury) are still in some of our vaccines. Other components such as egg, peanut, gluten, casein, and soy are used to form a hapten with the virus or bacteria and may also cause allergies.

Today the recommended vaccine schedule includes 81 vaccinations for a child from birth to age six! If a young child doesn't have the ability to detoxify the metals, everything that is injected stays in the child's tissues and, ultimately, their bones.

In combination, we are exposed to potentially harmful amounts of heavy metals through water and air contamination, deodorants and other personal care items, vaccines, and harmful dental fillings.

Following the Ten Commandments of Ultimate Health is crucial to cleansing the body of these toxins.

GETTING STARTED

The only way to tackle morbific stimuli is to make one change at a time. When I started working with Dr. Pitman, I thought, "There is no way I can do all of this." I started by purchasing only green products to clean my house and by attempting to purchase only high-quality organic foods.

Once organic foods and cleaners became a habit, I slowly started to combat the other morbific stimuli. I was amazed at how little changes, one by one, can add up to one big lifestyle change.

Every time I picked up the book to work on it, it seemed I became aware of another morbific stimulus that could be easily avoided. Usually, it was a fairly simple change. Things like buying a toaster oven to reduce microwave use, making a commitment to take my probiotic daily, and beginning to buy organic shampoo — all of these came fairly easily once I decided to do them.

Start by using the speaker phone on your cell phone, putting a piece of copper on the back of it, or having an old-fashioned home phone (with a cord) available for long conversations. Convert your metal pots into storage containers. Ask your dentist a few questions before your next *appointment.*

No matter what you choose to do for your first step, the important thing is that you take that first step, that you just get started!

"Therefore, I urge you, brothers and sisters, in view of God's mercy, to offer your bodies as a living sacrifice, holy and pleasing to God —this is your true and proper worship. Do not conform to the pattern of this world, but be transformed by renewing your mind. Then you will be able to test and approve what God's will is — his good, pleasing, and perfect will."

Romans 12:1, 2

REFERENCES

1. Devi S. Nambudripad, *Say Goodbye to Children's Allergies* (Buena Park, CA: Delta Publishers, 2001), 18.

2. John Cloud, "Why Your DNA Isn't Your Destiny," *Time* online, published January 6, 2010, http://www.time.com/time/magazine/article/0,9171,1952313,00.html (accessed October 15, 2011).

3. Ibid.

4. Ibid.

5. William J. Cromie, "One-Third of Americans Pray for Their Health—But Does It Make A Difference?" *Harvard Gazette*, May 13, 2004, http://www.news.harvard.edu/gazette/2004/05.13/01-prayer.html (accessed October 15, 2011).

6. Duke University, "Inorganic Elements in Tap Water," http://www.chem.duke.edu/~jds/cruise_chem/water/watinorg.html (accessed October 15, 2011).

7. Ibid.

8. "Prescription Drug Trends," The Henry J. Kaiser Foundation, June 2006, www.kff.org/rxdrugs/upload/3057-05.pdf (accessed October 15, 2011).

9. "Drugs in US Drinking Water," *Medical News Today*, March 10, 2008, http://www.medicalnewstoday.com/articles/100038.php (accessed October 15, 2011).

10. "Cocaine, Spices, Hormones Found In Drinking Water," *National Geographic Daily News*, http://news.nationalgeographic.com/news/2009/091112-drinking-water-cocaine/ (accessed December 2, 2011).

11. "Fluoride in Water Linked to Lower IQ in Children," PR Newswire, http://www.prnewswire.com/news-releases/fluoride-in-water-linked-to-lower (accessed October 15, 2011).

12. "Basic Information About Fluoride in Drinking Water," Environmental Protection Agency, http://water.epa.gov/drink/contaminants/basicinformation/fluoride.cfm (accessed October 15, 2011).

13. "Does Fluoride Really Fight Cavities by 'the Skin of the Teeth,'" *Science Daily*, Science News, http://www.sd.com/releases/2010/12/101215121918.htm (accessed January 4, 2012).

14. "Tox-Town: Environmental health concerns and toxic chemicals where you live, work, and play," National Library of Science, http://toxtown.nlm.nih.gov/text_version/chemicals.php?id=69 (accessed October 15, 2011).

15. "Teens and Mobile Phones," Pew Research Center, Pew Internet, http://www.pewinternet.org/Reports/2010/Teens-and-Mobile-Phones/Chapter-3/Sleeping-with-the-phone-on-or-near-the-bed.aspx (accessed October 14, 2011).

16. "Teens Sleeping with Cell Phones: A Clear and Present Danger," *This Emotional Life*/PBS Television, This Emotional Life Adolescence/Blog, http://www.pbs.org/thisemotionallife (accessed October 15, 2011).

17. "Information on Sleep Health and Safety," National Sleep Foundation, http://www.sleepfoundation.org/article/sleep-topics/depression-and-Sleep (accessed October 15, 2011).

18. Alexandros N. Vgontzas, Duanping Liao, Slobodanka Pejovic, Susan Calhoun, Maria Karataraki, Maria Basta, Julio Fernández-Mendoza, Edward O. Bixler, "Insomnia with Short Sleep Duration and Mortality: The Penn State Cohort," *SLEEP*, Vol. 33, No. 9, 2010.

19. Ibid., 17.

20. Michael Pollan, *In Defense of Food: An Eater's Manifesto* (New York, NY: Penguin, 2007), 1.

21. "Dietary Sugars Intake and Cardiovascular Health". Circulation 120:1011-1020 http://circ.ahajournals.org/content/120/11/1011.full.pdf (accessed 3/18/2012).

22. Pollan, *In Defense of Food: An Eater's Manifesto*, 147.

23. David Schardt, "It Was Forty Years Ago Today . . . " *Nutrition Action*, 38, no. 1 , January/February 2011, 10.

24.. "Profiling Food Consumption in America," United States Department of Agriculture, *Agriculture Fact Book 2001-2002*, http://www.usda.gov/factbook/chapter2.htm (accessed October 15, 2011).

25. Pollan, *In Defense of Food: An Eater's Manifesto*, 97.

26. "Diabetes Statistics—United States," Diabetes Partnership of Cleveland,

http://www.dagc.org/diastatsUS.asp (accessed October 15, 2011).

27. "What We Know About Childhood Obesity," American Public Health Association, http://www.apha.org/programs/resources/obesity/proresobesityknow.htm (accessed October 15, 2011).

28. Claudia Anrig, "Where's HFCS? It's Everywhere," *To Your Health*, January 2011.

29. Bruce West, "Poisoning Yourself So Sweetly: The Stealth Diseases," *Health Alert*, Volume 28, Issue 2 (February 2011), 1.

30. "Your Questions Answered," The Calorie Control Council, http://www.sucralose.org/questions/ (accessed October 15, 2011).

31. Schardt, 10.

32. "Changes in Midline-Crossing Inhibition in the Lower Extremities," *The Journals Of Gerontology*, Series A, 55, no.5 (1999), 294.

33. Min Lee, "Exercise Intensity and Longevity in Men," *Journal of American Medical Association*, 273, no. 15 (1995), 1180.

34. R.W. Bryner and R.C. Toffle, "The Effects of Exercise Intensity on Body Composition, Weight Loss, and Dietary Composition in Women," *Journal of the American College of Nutrition*, 16, no. 1 (February 1997), 71.

35. American College of Sports Medicine, "Physical Activity & Public Health Guidelines," American College of Sports Medicine Physical Activity Guidelines, http://www.acsm.org/AM/PrinterTemplate.cfm?Section=Home_Page&TEMPLATE=CM (accessed October 15, 2011).

36. Cellerciser, "Cellercise . . . The Ultimate Exercise," The Official Cellerciser, http://www.cellerciser.com/ (accessed October 15, 2011).

37. Jack Lalanne, "Lalanneisms," http://www.jacklalanne.com/jacks-adventures/lalanneisms.php (accessed October 14, 2011).

38. Ibid.

39. Cancer Prevention Coalition, "Carcinogens at Home," http://www.preventcancer.com/consumers/household/carcinogens_home.htm (accessed October 14, 2011).

40. Google, "80,000 Synthetic Chemicals Registered for Use in U.S," http://www.google.com/search?hl=en&source=hp&q=80%2c000+synthetic+c

hecmicals+registered+for+use+in+u.s. (accessed October 15, 2011).

41. Nikolas R. Hedberg, "Thyroid Disrupting Chemicals," *The Original Internist* (March 2011) .

42. Lisa Moran, "The 5 Most Popular Supplements," *Prevention*, February 4, 2011.

43. Consumer Lab, "Multivitamin and Multi-mineral Supplements Review," http://www.consumerlab.com/.

44. Robert H. Fletcher and Kathleen M. Fairfield, "Vitamins for Chronic Disease Prevention in Adults," T*he Journal of the American Medical Association*, 287, no. 23 (2002): 3127-3129.

45. David Schardt, "Achoo! How to Avoid Catching a Cold," *Nutrition Action*, 38, no. 2 (March 2011): 8.

46. David Perlmutter, "Human Memory: Why Bad Memories Stick," The Huffington Post, http://www.huffingtonpost.com/dr-david-perlmutter-md/human-memory-why-do-we_b_808909.html (accessed March 22, 2012).

47. Ibid.

48. Ibid.

49. Laura Story lyrics and music, "Blessings," Columbia/INO, from the album, "Blessings" (2011).

50. Robert W. Sears MD, FAAP, *The Vaccine Book: Making the Right Decision for Your Child* (USA, Little Brown and Company, Hachette Book Group, 2007), 17.

51. Ibid.

52. National Institutes of Health, "Impairing Oral Tolerance Promotes Allergy and Anaphylaxis: A New Murine Food Allergy Model," NIH Public Access Author Manuscript, http://www.ncbi.nlm.nih.gov/pmc/articles/PMC2787105/ (accessed December 3, 2011).

53. David Rich, *Food, Inc.*, DVD, directed by Robert Kenner (New York, New York: Magnolia Pictures, 2009).

54. Ohio Citizen Action, "Lanxess Plastics–Addyston," http://www.ohiocitizen.org/campaigns/bayer/bayer.html (accessed October 14, 2007).

55. Food Inc., "Hungry for a Change Food, Inc." http://www.foodincmovie.com/hungry-for-change-cafetaria.php (accessed January 12, 2009).

56. Gordon Shetler, "Farm Pesticides Linked to Deadly Skin Cancer," *Environmental Health News*, March 31, 2010.

57. Ibid.

58. Environmental Working Group, "EWG's Shopper's Guide to Pesticides in Produce," http://www.ewg.org/foodnews/ (accessed October 14, 2011).

59. Pollan, *In Defense of Food: An Eater's Manifesto*, 157.

60. Mercola, "What You Don't Know About Flavor Enhancers Can Harm You," Mercola.com, http://articles.mercola.com/sites/articles/archive/2011/09/01/what-you-don't-know-about-flavor-enhancers-can-harm-you (accessed October 14, 2011).

61. Weston A. Price Foundation, "Senomyx," http://www.westonaprice.org/modern-foods/senomyx (accessed March 22, 2012).

62. Mercola, 60.

63. Schardt, "It Was Forty Years Ago Today . . . " : 10.

64. Oregon Department of Environmental Quality, "Household Hazardous Waste Program" http://www.deq.state.or.us/lq/sw/hhw/index.htm (accessed January 22, 2012).

65. U.S. Consumer and Product Safety Commission, "Chemical Industry Test Results Show Formaldehyde Has Caused Cancer in Lab Animals," News from Consumer Product Safety Commission, http://www.cpsc.gov/CPSCPUB/PREREL/prhtml79/79059.html (accessed October 4, 2011).

66. Canadian Broadcasting Corporation, "If You Can't Pronounce It, Should You Use It?," *Marketplace*, CBC Marketplace: Household Cleaners, http://www.health-report.co.uk/toxic_household_chemicals.htm (accessed March 22, 2012).

67. Environmental Working Group, "In Depth: Common Ingredients to Avoid," Skin Deep Cosmetics Database, http://www.ewg.org/skindeep/top-tips-for-safer-products/ (accessed October 14, 2011).

68. Ibid.

69. Rash Bihari Dubey, Madasu Hanmandlu, and Suresh Kumar Gupta, "Risk

of Brain Tumors from Wireless Phone Use," *Journal Of Computer Assisted Tomography* 34, no.6 (November/December 2010): 804.

70. Mercola, "Why You Should Avoid Root Canals Like the Plague," Mercola.com, http://articles.mercola.com/sites/articles/archive/2010/11/16/why-you-should-avoid (accessed October 14, 2011).

71. Independent Cancer Research Foundation, Inc., "The Relationship Between Root Canals and Cancer," http://new-cancer-Treatments.org/Articles/RootCanals.html (accessed March 22, 2012).

ABOUT THE AUTHORS

Dr. Greg Pitman, DC, DNBHE

Dr. Greg Pitman is a chiropractor, homeopath, and natural medicine practitioner. His waiting room is filled with patients who have not been helped by conventional medicine and are seeking healing. In his 28 years of practice, he has helped thousands of individuals battling a wide variety of illnesses. He is committed to finding and treating the underlying cause of his patients' ailments and leading them towards a healthier lifestyle.

Dr. Pitman's quest to understand the human body began when he was a young boy and continues today. After graduating from Bluffton College and Palmer Chiropractic College, he engaged in extensive international travel, searching for comprehensive treatments that addressed the whole person –physically, emotionally, and spiritually. He has studied under acclaimed teachers such as Dr. George Goodheart, Dr. Victor Frank, Dr. Alexander Wood and Helman Schimal and continued his education by obtaining his Diplomate of the National Board of Homeopathic Examiners.

As a successful practitioner and national speaker, Dr. Pitman was compelled to write a comprehensive guide that could help even more people achieve a healthier life. This guide is *The Ten Commandments of Ultimate Health*.

Dr. Pitman serves on the Board of Energetix. He lives in Cincinnati, Ohio with his wife Donna and three children.

Lynn Thesing

Lynn Thesing enjoyed a successful career as a sales director for a Fortune 500 company when she was called to serve in the not-for-profit sector. She became the Executive Director of Starfire in Cincinnati for eight years, where she was an award winning grant writer. In 2008, she left Starfire to answer an even greater calling: to try to heal her two very sick children that were plagued by allergies, asthma, and learning issues.

For months, Lynn researched medical options for her children, resulting in an extensive schedule of doctor and therapy appointments. When she finally sent her children to Dr. Pitman and began to see results immediately, she became committed to spreading the word about these beneficial treatments. As the co-author of *The Ten Commandments of Ultimate Health*, Lynn creatively guides the reader through steps to healthier living, utilizing recent research, everyday experiences, testimonials, and practical advice.

Lynn is a graduate of the University of Cincinnati. She is the also the author of the upcoming children's book, *Water- the Coolest Drink Around*. She currently lives in the greater Cincinnati area with her husband and her two healthy children.